Renewing your *Spiritual Passion*

GORDON
MacDONALD

OLIVER
NELSON

THOMAS NELSON PUBLISHERS
Nashville • Atlanta • London • Vancouver

Published in Nashville, Tennessee, by Thomas Nelson, Inc., Publishers, and distributed in Canada by Word Communications, Ltd., Richmond, British Columbia.

Scripture quotations marked RSV are from the REVISED STANDARD VERSION of the Bible. Copyright 1946, 1952, 1971, 1973 by the Division of Christian Education of the National Council of Churches of Christ. Used by permission.

Scripture quotations marked TEV are from Today's English Version—Old Testament: Copyright © American Bible Society 1976, 1992: New Testament: Copyright © American Bible Society 1966, 1971, 1976, 1992. Used by permission.

Scripture quotations marked TLB are taken from *The Living Bible,* copyright 1971 by Tyndale House Publishers, Wheaton, IL. Used by permission.

Scripture quotations marked NIV are taken from the HOLY BIBLE: NEW INTERNATIONAL VERSION ®. Copyright © 1973, 1978, 1984 by the International Bible Society. Used by permission of Zondervan Publishing House. All rights reserved.

Library of Congress Cataloging-in-Publication Data

MacDonald, Gordon.
    Renewing your spiritual passion / Gordon MacDonald.
        p. cm. — (The Gordon MacDonald bestseller series)
    Originally published: Oliver-Nelson, 1989.
    Includes bibliographical references.
    ISBN   0-7852-7162-7 (pb.)
    1. Christian life.   I. Title.   II. Series.
[BV4501.2.M22738   1997]
248.4—dc21   97-6544
                                                                            CIP

Printed in the United States of America.

8 9 10 11 12 13 14 15 16 17—01 00 99 98 97

CONTENTS

PREFACE

The Dark-Road
Times

Within the kaleidoscope of my distorted childhood memories is the image of a dusty, deserted road in rural Canada. As I recall it, there were no signs indicating direction or distance to go, and the route itself was not marked on my father's map.

The hour was late, and my family and I had been traveling that road for an entire day. We were lost, tired, and not a little irritable with one another. Those were not the days of frequently seen motels, and the few (very few) collections of cabins along the way displayed NO VACANCY signs to fend away further inquiries.

Why not turn back? We had simply traveled too far to do so. Besides, the road had to go somewhere. But why keep going? That was the purpose of the trip: to get somewhere. Surely there would be a place ahead where we could find food and rest. So we pushed ahead. The world was not flat; we would not drop off an edge, although my childish perspective contemplated the possibility. We had to be going somewhere. But where?

The trip had begun with such excitement, an adventuresome spirit about going new places. Most vacation trips begin that way. The car had been packed with care, maps marked, a picnic basket prepared. But now all that zeal had dissipated. I guess we began to wonder why we'd ever left home.

I have often recalled the feelings and frustration of that late-night, dark-road experience whenever my life seemed to momentarily turn into a mindless or spiritless journey crammed with events (not experiences) and contacts (not relationships). In such confounding periods my sense is that one feels like my family did that night in Canada. Where is all of this going? What does it mean? And how will I know when the destination has been reached? Why has this exciting trip suddenly turned into a wearisome journey? When will I find tranquillity again?

To claim that such questions do not occur to a Christian is to be unrealistic and, I might add, unhelpful. For most of us such questions come and come often, and for those few who deny it, I will offer them the benefit of the doubt.

I think Simon Peter was in the middle of one those dark-road times when he said to his friends, "I am going fishing," and they said, "We're going with you." My bet is that Peter was on the edge of exhaustion—physical, spiritual, and psychic. Too many new and stressful things had been happening to the premier disciple: Judas' surprising betrayal of the Lord, Peter's shocking three-time denial of association with Christ, the subsequent trial, the crucifixion, and the resurrection appearances.

The inner personal world of Peter could absorb just so much, and although we could reason that he should have been ready to take it all in and respond with ease, he wasn't. In a kind of numbness he withdrew to the only thing he really knew how to do with certainty: making money catching fish. Perhaps familiarity would restore whatever it was that was lost deep within.

Using Peter's approach, my family would have turned

back on that lonely road—back to something familiar where we could get our bearings again, back to a point where we could gain some degree of control over the hours, the energies, and the direction.

Peter's personal struggle with a sort of weariness did not go on indefinitely. With manly gestures and words, Jesus Christ did a beautiful thing for the exhausted, unproductive fisherman.

What were the gestures? He built a fire, cooked a breakfast, and invited Peter to join him.

What were the words? The ones Christ chose siphoned off the pain of guilt, the embarrassment of failure, and the confusion of mixed motives and goals. Then He repainted the big picture of the original call to servanthood so that Peter was able to function again. What was the result? He restored Peter's spiritual passion. And that's what needs to happen to all of us with regularity.

For some time I have sensed that many people claiming a Christian commitment are careening down an unmarked road of life, a road something like the one in my childhood experience. We believe that the road is going somewhere, but we're not sure where that somewhere is or how we will be certain when we've reached the destination. In transit we move at a dangerous kind of top speed, because we think that that will quicken the time of arrival. And with every mile we may grow increasingly frustrated and tired.

Occasionally we hear of fellow travelers on that same road who crash, and we wonder why they were not smart enough to keep in the lane. Others simply seem to disappear as if they had driven off on a side road and found another direction. But the majority keep pressing on ahead unable to turn back but unsure of what's ahead. And the further they go, the more weary they become.

This weariness is a far cry from the excitement that usually marks the beginning of a trip. What happens? What goes wrong?

Renewing Your Spiritual Passion is meant to take a look at the journey we are on as Christians. A traveler for many years, I've looked into my own experiences and those of others to determine what it is that often adds fatigue and weariness to the trip. I've wanted to catalog some of the issues that slowly drain off the zeal and threaten to leave us with a loss of heart.

I've chosen the word *passion* when others might have used words like *power, zeal, enthusiasm,* or maybe even *joy.* All of these words, and many others like them, speak to the sort of inner force that God promised and that many testify to having received.

Who of us does not crave the passion or the power to be godly people? to give witness to our faith? to serve and give selflessly? to own control of our drives and dispositions? But for many it is easier to talk about passion than to find it or, having found it, to maintain it.

A friend of mine once had a serious struggle with cancer. I asked her one day if her pastor brought help to her when he came to visit her in the hospital. "I'd rather he not come," she said, "because when he visits, he tells me how I ought to feel rather than ask how I actually do feel."

Not only was her comment a lesson to me about how to treat suffering people, but it also reminded me of my own attitude when others have come along with a view of spiritual passion or energy that I was supposed to embrace *because* it had worked for them. As a young man I must have tried a dozen techniques that people said were sure to guarantee a measure of passion that would transport me above the ordinary and ineffective. In each case I eagerly em-

8

braced whatever it was that I was supposed to do or say. But the results, if any, were short-lived, and what I discovered was that there are no shortcuts, no gimmicks, no easy ways to cultivate an intimacy with God and attain the resulting passion that should carry one through life's journey.

Then slowly it dawned on me that I and scores of others were paying a terrible price for this search for some magical breakthrough. We were trying harder, working longer, breathing heavier, and getting wearier. And it was an unpleasant journey when it shouldn't have been. Other words that describe such a trip are *sour, stale, bored,* and *numb.* We would never have admitted it, but we were tired of God, of faith, and of faith's people. Now, how could a call to abundant living turn into such dullness of spirit? That we should tire of Him was not God's fault. Rather this weariness calls into question the system of spirituality many of us have been taught.

Although the Scriptures frequently describe some tremendous breakthrough in the spiritual performance of a prophet or apostolic personality, I'd like to suggest that the action is not really there. What we have not stopped to think about is the many long hours and days between the major moments of performance. For example, we know barely a handful of the special moments in the life of the apostle Paul. What we need to ask is how did the man live in the times not recorded in the Scriptures. His attitudes and actions at such times probably have more to tell us about normal spiritual life than the great moments of which Luke wrote.

I want to confess that I have struggled more with the writing of this book than with any I have ever written. First, I found it hard to deal on paper with my own failings and frustrations. But I felt that I had to because whenever I have allowed some personal transparency or vulnerability, I have connected with scores of other people who were thankful to discover that they were not alone. Second, I'm embarrassed with the simple and the "un-novel" nature of my thoughts. Third, I struggle every day (let me repeat: every day!) to put these principles in which I believe to work in my own experience. How I wish I could write from a richer, deeper, more experienced heart!

What compels me to write about the renewal of spiritual passion? I write because I sense out there in the real world of Western Christians that there is a growing weariness of spirit. We have tried the gimmicks, the programs, the promises of a thousand and one "gurus" of the faith. Here and there one view or another seems to catch on. But for many, the journey is a boresome task, and like my family on the dark road, we can't turn back, but we're almost too tired to go on.

Renewing Your Spiritual Passion is disarmingly simple. I merely want to ask the question, what are the things that tire us out and drain us of our desire to be people of God? Let's name the issues and face them squarely for what they are. Then let's ask, how did men and women of spiritual antiquity face these same agents of weariness? Did they have insights we've ignored? And finally, what difference would it make if we followed their advice? My guess is that we would find some ways not only to restore spiritual passion but also to maintain some of the passion we still have.

At least that's the way it seems to me.

Gordon MacDonald
Canterbury, New Hampshire
Madison, Wisconsin

10

1

It's Got to Glow in You All the Time

He was the first professional athlete I had ever known personally. And in his prime as a football player he was an all-pro pass defender, the best in his business. Like many other people, I was drawn to him, to the force within him that made him a winner, a man with the courage to put his body on the line against an opponent before 75,000 people.

On a Monday, six days before his team would play against the Dallas Cowboys, the two of us were having lunch together. The upcoming game was the subject of our conversation. "How will you prepare yourself for the Cowboy pass offense?" I asked him. "What will your schedule be this week?"

"Well the mornings will all be practice at the stadium," he answered. "And then I'll go home to my den and load the projector [these were the days before VCR's] with game films, and I'll study the Cowboy receivers until I know all of them better than their wives do. I'll check every movement they make when they come out of the huddles to see if they reveal what sort of play it's going to be, what pattern they're going to run, or whether or not they're going to stay back and block."

"What about your evenings?" I asked.

"Oh, I'll keep watching those films straight through until midnight every night."

"Ten hours a day? All week? Nothing else?" I was incredulous.

"Easily," he responded. "Hey, I want to beat those men. I want to hit them so hard if they come into my zone that when they're lying on the ground, they'll look up to the sky with glassy eyes and pray that there won't have to be another play in the game. I want to totally dominate their spirits."

That's passion speaking! Extreme, powerful passion! That's one brand of passion, but there are other brands. The kind I've described may even repel some of us because we could never be so intense and because we do not feel comfortable around people with such intensity. And that's OK.

I only know that when I saw my friend's passion to win a football game (the score and winner of which I cannot even remember), I was inwardly embarrassed to realize that there was no part of my life where I could say I was paying a similar price: not in my family life, not in my work, not in the pursuit of my faith.

Why? I asked myself.

I was bothered that I had no adequate answer.

It certainly is mysterious, this word *passion*. It is hard to measure and difficult to pin down. But you know when you have it, and you are quite aware when you don't. One feels passion; it seizes you! Passion stimulates human performance: superior or excellent performance, strange or bizarre performance, compassionate or sacrificial performance.

We identify passion with romance, revolution, extraordinary achievement, and violence. We use it to explain actions we don't understand. All we know is that it appears to be a force within people that moves them beyond ordinary human activities. Some would suggest that almost all the great literature, drama, and music feature the tale of passion in all its grand forms.

Passion in me seems to be selective. I would like to think I'm passionate when it comes to hugging my wife. I think I've sensed a bit of passion when I have been speaking to a crowd of people on certain subjects that grip my imagination or my sense of outrage. I can get passionate about something I'm writing, and once this fascinating force gains control, I can sit at the keyboard of my computer utterly oblivious of the passing hours as I play with words and phrases to make my point.

On the other hand I'm not inclined, like some, to act out of passionate anger. That is not a virtue, understand; it is merely a segment of my natural temperament. Then, too, I find it difficult to commit to a plethora of causes and movements as a few of my acquaintances do. For me even a passionate expression of belief comes hard. Perhaps that is why I'm uncomfortable with Simon Peter (who is passionate no matter what the issue) and sympathetic to Thomas (the doubter? or merely the cautious one?) when I ponder the temperaments of the disciples of our Lord.

It's hard for me to remember when passion first became an issue for me. I think it was sometime in my college years. I have a recollection of sitting as a graduate student in a seminar room at the University of Colorado. About the table were a dozen men and women, all, like myself, in hot pursuit of a doctorate degree in history. On the table were stacks of books, index cards containing bibliographical notes, and pads upon which we jotted notes from the discussion. The topic was the economic impact of the changes in tobacco prices in the Virginia Colony of the seventeenth century. That afternoon there were differing opinions.

The conversation grew hotter and hotter as various students offered their interpretations of the matter at hand. People raced through books or cards, looking for the one piece of evidence that would substantiate their view of the situation. Voice decibels were raised; hands forcefully gestured; gasps of disgust became frequent as disagreement gained momentum. Everyone was intensely involved, except me.

I drifted away from the vigorous exchanges and began to listen from another perspective, one that did not search for the right interpretation to the problem of Virginia's colonial economy. I'm sure I'd seen passion before, but this was the first time I'd actually attempted to analyze it.

These students really cared about this subject. And I didn't! They appeared prepared to come close to physical blows to defend their opinion. I wasn't! Was this the sort of internal energy that it took to gain a research doctorate? Was this what some meant when they talked about passionate commitment?

I had to conclude that I didn't have passion. At least not for the destabilizing effect of changing tobacco prices. And when I left the room that day, I never went back. It was pointless, I concluded, to commit to an all-consuming goal for which I had no passion.

That was the day I learned that the people in our world who rise to the top of business, sports, academia, science, and politics usually do it because they are fueled by passion. It could be a passion for power, notoriety, or raw achievement. But whatever the motive, a brand of passion is called into action. When I saw the passion of my friend the football player who was preparing for the Dallas Cowboys, I

14

recalled the energy I'd seen in that graduate seminar room at the University of Colorado.

Another athlete, Bart Starr, former quarterback of the world champion Green Bay Packers, talked about one of the most passionate men ever associated with professional football, Vincent Lombardi:

> I wasn't mentally tough before I met Coach Lombardi. I hadn't reached the point where I refused to accept second best. I was too nice at times. I don't believe that nice guys necessarily finish last. I think what Leo Durocher really meant is that nice guys don't finish first. To win, you have to have a certain amount of mental toughness. Coach Lombardi gave me that. *He taught me that you must have a flaming desire to win. It's got to dominate all your waking hours. It can't ever wane. It's got to glow in you all the time* (Kramer, *Lombardi*, p. 86, emphasis mine).

"It's got to glow in you," Starr says. What glows? Passion, the flaming desire. And it glows "all the time." That's a big order, probably an impossibility. But even in his exaggeration, Bart Starr is telling us something of the curious stuff within people who want to be a part of the extraordinary in this world, the folk who change things, make statements, move people, do great things for God.

The prize fighter refers to passion as a killer instinct, the way of the hungry boxer. The businessperson thinks of passion when speaking of an eye for the top. The academic might call it the unvarnished quest for truth. The soldier speaks of gung-ho, and the artist of a kind of mystical perfection.

I think my mother was operating from passion when she did not hesitate to get up in the middle of the night and tend to me when I was a sick child. Passion excited her "mother's ear," and it became sensitive, it seemed, to the slightest change in my breathing or to my most feeble call from two rooms away.

With such terms and performance patterns, people are telling us what passion means in one form or another.

Passion—the kind that causes some to excel beyond anyone else—dulls one's sense of fatigue, pain, and the need for pleasure or even well-being. Passion leads some to pay incredible prices to reach a goal of some sort.

Paul spoke from a wellspring of passion when he wrote: "But one thing I do, forgetting what lies behind and straining forward to what lies ahead, I press on toward the goal for the prize of the upward call of God in Christ Jesus" (Phil. 3:13–14 RSV).

A passion is necessary in the performance of Christian faith. When Athanasius, the early church father, was told by his judge that the whole world was against him, Athanasius responded passionately, "Then is Athanasius against the whole world." And Luther had to be operating from internal passion when he stood before the intimidating power of the papal legates from Rome and said, "Here I stand; I can do nothing else." And Jim Elliot was clearly in the grip of a passion when he and his missionary team set their tiny plane down in a jungle area renowned for murderous Aucas.

Some of us experience another form of passion when we first make a decision to cross a descision line and commit to Jesus Christ. Most of us have seen the new believer who—like the healed man in the temple of Jerusalem—leaps for joy and cares little about what anyone thinks because he is so excited about a new life. So strong is that initial passion that it is almost embarrassing to those who have had more

16

experience in matters of faith, who have a larger perspective.

"He'll quiet down," they say, because they know. Or at least they think they know that the initial surge of energy cannot last forever and that it will one day be diminished by a more realistic view of things.

But true Christian maturity does not preclude passion. Perhaps a more experienced style of faith may appear to be controlled or channeled a bit as when engineers redirect a peaking flood. And that may be important to remember, because we tend to conclude that a mature faith does not give way to explosions of joy or to commitments to objectives that defy the rational mind.

Years after the conversation with my friend the football player, I sat at another lunch with still another friend, who matched my age. We had shared similar life and faith styles. Our backgrounds had caused us to know the Bible well, to make fellowship with Christians an important element of life, and to make doing Christian things a priority. But as we talked, I could tell that my friend bordered on boredom as he told about certain activities in his church, and I decided to penetrate the cloud cover of religious jargon.

"Where are you at these days with God," I asked, using the same, casual tone of voice I would have used to ask about the Dow Jones averages.

"Where am I at with God?" he repeated the question as he looked off at a 45-degree angle from me. There was at least a 30-second pause, and I decided to wait it out. "Do you really want to know?" he finally asked.

"Yeah, I'm your friend, and I'm interested," I responded.

"I'm not anywhere," he said, "and I haven't been anywhere for a long time. When it comes to my Christian life,

17

I'm going through the motions." I made a mental note to ponder his meaning. His comment suggested that there was a sector in his world called the Christian life and that there were other sectors that were some other sort of life.

"Gordon, there was a time in my younger years when it all seemed to grab my imagination, Christ and faith, I mean. I really wanted to make my Christian commitment the absolute center of everything. But I've lost it, and so now I perform more out of habit than anything else."

"What drives you to keep on with the habits?" I probed.

"I suppose only the fact that I'm getting to the point in life where it's too late to change. My family life is all centered on Christian activities, and I don't want to hurt my wife or the kids. And besides, life has been good to me. Why upset the routines that have gotten me this far? So I just keep chugging along."

I had heard this sort of observation before. In fact, I've heard it in discussions with pastors, with missionaries, with lay leaders in churches, with the common man who always seems to be in the midst of things whenever church groups are together.

What's missing? Probably passion! And why is it missing? Usually people don't know. They suddenly become aware, if they have the courage to evaluate inwardly (not many do), that there is no longer an energy to their faith experience. Or they realize that their energy has been reallocated toward the pursuit of a career position or toward a hobby or recreational effort or toward some activity that appears more daring, more pleasurable, or more personally affirming.

And once they get involved with alternatives to spiritual passion, Chrisitan activity becomes dull and boring. They are either beset by guilt or numbed to spiritual sensitivities.

The opposite, of course, is the person who has found a way to maintain such a passion. One is impressed with the words of Willard Hotchkiss, a pioneer missionary who served in Africa who, looking back over a long life of service, wrote:

> I have dwelt forty years practically alone in Africa. I have been 39 times stricken with the fever, three times attacked by lions, and several times by rhinoceri; but let me say to you, I would gladly go through the whole thing again, if I could have the joy of again bringing that word "Savior" and flashing it into the darkness that envelopes another tribe in Central Africa (Hefley and Hefley, *By Their Blood,* p. 340).

Now that's passion! It easily matches that of my friend the pass defender. But it's another brand of passion that probably wouldn't impress my lunch companion either. "You know, that's one of the problems that has always bugged me," he said. "People keep quoting someone else— who usually lives far, far away or who lived in another generation—and say in effect, 'Why can't you be like him?' You know what effect it has on me? I just get more and more miserable when I'm asked to live up to someone else. I'm not them, and they're not me. I used to feel guilty and try to conjure up some feelings when I was challenged like that, and sometimes I could actually do it for a while. Then I gave up. So when those sorts of conversations start, I just turn off."

As a young person I remember many drives along the western banks of New York's Hudson River. Some miles north of the city was an anchorage where dozens of World War II liberty ships were tied side by side. They floated lifelessly, silently, in—as they say—mothballs.

I remember those ships that once sailed the wartime oceans filled with the fuel, the munitions, the supplies that would launch an army toward the heart of the Axis empire. I used to ponder the hostile action they had seen, the drama that must have taken place as they faced the enemy submarines and aircraft. It had been an era of bravery and valor, of action and productivity.

But now, here on the Hudson, the holds were empty, the decks stripped of their guns and armor. The engines were silent; the crews were scattered. The ships were like floating tombs.

Was that the case of the man who sat with me at lunch and had the courage to describe a real-life situation? I suspect it was.

Can the ships be reclaimed? Brought back to productivity? Of course. Unfortunately—and here the parable begins to disintegrate—some of them will become so useless that they will be towed to sea and sunk, if not torn apart for the scrap heap.

What would it take for my friend to renew the spiritual passion of an earlier time? Could he return to a point in the spiritual formation of his life where he could begin a growth track again? Could he resurrect some sense of affection for God and God's activities?

My friend is not an evil man intent upon destroying the world around him. In fact he is a very good man: a loving husband and father, a loyal contributor to his business, a basic asset to his community. He's a very normal man who'd like to go beyond his present limits, but isn't; and doesn't see how it could ever be different or better.

How might he renew that spiritual passion of earlier days? Perhaps it would be good, first of all, if he understood the many and varied ways that such passion is diminished to the point of nonexistence.

Then it might be helpful if he thought through the simple disciplines that aerate the inner spirit from which this kind of passion flows. It's possible, just possible, that spiritual passion could be restored. And if it could be restored for him, why could it not for millions of others who call themselves Christians but sense deep within that what they are into is more habit than passion.

Masculine drives within me cause me to admire the football player who wants to win so badly that he'll pay the price. But the more I think about it, I admire an even deeper quality about him. Even though a few people might think he's committed to something quite senseless, at least in contrast to the larger issues of life, he is a person committed to something. He knows the feeling of being lifted above ordinary limitations. He understands what it is like to be singularly focused. He appreciates the meaning of risk for something he perceives as larger than himself.

Something in me admires that. Something inside me wants to know it is possible to generate that kind of passion and, if my spiritual passion ever gets dissipated, to know it is possible to renew it. Something prods me to think that the drive that generates that kind of passion can generate a spiritual passion that can lift me to an extraordinary service for God and His people, a passion that does more than win games. It could be an energy that changes things in my little world.

2
Doing More and Enjoying It Less

I'm not sure I understand it, but I have this feeling that an increasing amount of conversational time between friends is spent on the subject of weariness, overcommitment, the perceived need to drop out.

You see someone you know, and you ask a simple question: "What's going on in your world these days?"

You may get an all too common answer: "I've got to cut down! I'm in to too many things."

Or you ask someone how he or she is feeling and you're liable to hear the response, "I think I'm on the edge of burnout . . . or something."

You comment on how busy the last few weeks seem to have been, and someone agrees and begins to philosophize: "Tell me, do you ever ask yourself why we're doing all of this anyway?"

Or, being sensitive to someone who appears to have been working too hard, you remark, "You look like you're bushed tonight," and you hear, "I'm absolutely exhausted. I've never been so shot. I'll never get so overinvolved again."

Why on the one Sunday in five years when a New England snowstorm forced us to close down our church was it universally recognized by the congregation as the most wonderful Lord's day they had ever had? What was being said?

"I couldn't believe it," someone commented about the day. "I had an entire twenty-four hours with my family; no schedule, nothing to do, just being quiet. It was marvelous." I remember hearing that observation and wondering why we needed an "act of God" to force us into doing what we all badly wanted to do: enjoy with those whom we love an interlude in the schedule away from all the routine busyness. Strange! These were not spiritual rebels speaking. These were substantial, faithful people.

An old cigarette ad sums up these reactions quite well: "smoking more and enjoying it less." That is exactly what appears to be happening today among many people who have honestly tried to think and act toward the goal of making a contribution to their worlds—their churches, their communities, and other organizations.

We're talking about people with a vision to be useful. They are living according to the principle of responsibility, the belief that they have a contribution to make, that their generation ought to be just a little bit better because of who they are and what they are able to do. They see their abilities and energies as something they must share with others or with the organization of which they are a part. But the more willing they are to get involved, the more opportunities, sometimes even demands, seem to come their way.

What is the possible result? Increasing fatigue, exhaustion, weariness, loss of passion. Not necessarily of the body but of the spirit within. Sometimes you can almost see an erosion of the original excitement and joy begin to set in. And finally, if nothing is done to bring the process of busyness under discipline, the inner weariness begins to show in the quality of outer activity. Suddenly there is a surprising

23

sloppiness and undependability in the work. Irritations with people lead to conflicts. There may be physical sickness, a bitter spirit, and, finally, a crisis moment when one simply quits.

More and more we see people who were in the center of things one year suddenly drift away to the edge of things the next year and then quietly disappear to a more private life. Talk with them, and you discover that they came to a point where they lost their zeal to keep going. "I found myself chasing my tail around the proverbial barn," one woman said to me. "I was tired of being tired all the time."

From Mrs. Lettie Cowman's wonderful book, *Springs in the Valley* (pp. 196–97), comes this interesting tale from African colonial history:

In the deep jungles of Africa, a traveler was making a long trek. Coolies had been engaged from a tribe to carry the loads. The first day they marched rapidly and went far. The traveler had high hopes of a speedy journey. But the second morning these jungle tribesmen refused to move. For some strange reason they just sat and rested. On inquiry as to the reason for this strange behavior, the traveler was informed that they had gone too fast the first day, and that *they were now waiting for their souls to catch up with their bodies.*

Then Mrs. Cowman concludes with this penetrating exhortation:

This whirling rushing life which so many of us live does for us what that first march did for those poor jungle tribesmen. The difference: *they knew* what they needed to restore life's balance; too often *we do not.*

24

It is incredible to realize that Lettie Cowman wrote these words almost fifty years ago.

The way we get consumed by a schedule of activities suddenly out of control is alarming. It reminds one of the old Uncle Remus story of the tar baby. Hit the figure of tar with one fist, and your hand is stuck. So you hit it with the other in order to get unstuck, and you know what happens. Now you are in real trouble. Kick it with a free foot, and things get increasingly complicated. Use the last free limb, and the tar baby has got you. Sometimes I think modern schedules are like tar babies.

The analogy is a real one to me. I can easily recall the many times when I have accumulated a list of commitments and obligations (all perfectly good) that have made me feel as constrained as if I'd hit and kicked that tar baby.

The list had grown usually because the things asked of me were good things: challenging, needs-oriented things I believed God had equipped and gifted me to do. But at other times? I probably said yes and made the list grow because I wanted people to like me, because I didn't have the courage to say no, because I didn't want to be left out or because there was a stream of guilt (false guilt perhaps) that drowned out the voice of inner wisdom.

And what is the result when the list gets larger than life? It is weariness, the feeling of being trapped, the desire to run. This sort of thing is being expressed when one friend says to another, "You know, I used to enjoy doing this, but it isn't fun anymore."

The good news of modern busyness is the amazing outburst of opportunities to exercise our capacities and skills, our gifts and visions. The bad news is the increasing amount of fatigue and frustration in the spirit, the sense of a personal performance for God that is not spontaneous but rather too automatic, a joyless merry-go-round of activity that never seems to stop.

For those in the salaried Christian ministry, life usually revolves around a never-ending workcycle that is hard to interrupt without a sense of dis-ease about things still undone. Anyone who has given themselves to the leading, caring, or developing of people knows that there is always one more thing that could be done better and more completely.

For the layperson who seeks a faithful life for God in the church and in the marketplace, it would seem as if there is a relentless barrage of good things in which to be involved over and above the responsibilities for which one gets paid. "I do have a living to make and a family to support, you know," a layman said to me once when I had suggested one more thing he could do in the church.

Funny! It was as if that hadn't occurred to me. But the fact is if you do a few things well in any voluntary organization like the church, it will suddenly seem as if interesting folk come out of the wall with potential additions to the agenda or schedule. Doing one thing seems to lead to another. One is never sure when enough is enough.

In the religious world we are all confronted with a whirl of programs, conferences, seminars, and retreats inside and outside the church. The competition for our time and energy grows more fierce with each year and every bright person who has a new idea about something for us to learn or master. (I saw one seminar brochure recently with a money-back guarantee on the registration form: "If you don't agree that this is the most valuable seminar you've attended this year . . .")

How has this happened? It's the result of lots of good

26

things happening to us—innovation, visionary people, techniques and methods borrowed from every sector of modern life.

Weariness comes not only in the things there are to do but also from the incredible amount of experience and information coming at us. I think one can actually grow tired from the constant onrush of spiritual stimulation. Words and more words, sensation and excitement!

Christian media—radio and TV, the publishing empires, and the authors of direct mail—have all romanced us with an avalanche of causes and concerns asking for our money, our time and effort, and our loyalty. Using the most persuasive marketing techniques, the most attractive people, and the most heart-gripping stories, they claw at our emotions and our minds. They invite us to telethons, tours to the Holy Land, cruises in the Caribbean, banquets and retreats. It's not all bad. In fact, it can all be exciting—at first. But, like an addiction, we must experience more and more of it lest it grow weak and lose its ability to stimulate our passion. And it does have a wearying effect.

Most of us have forgotten the era in which the local Christian congregation had a very few basic programs aside from worship on Sunday morning. The modern program explosion has raised our expectations as well as our frustrations. Most of us would feel that we had been cheated or that our church was not keeping up with the times if there were not something going on every day and evening of the week to meet the expanded sense of human need and desire to be doing everything. But of course those busy programs need personnel both to run them and to participate in them. And you know who that is.

An associate of mine is fond of comparing situations in which one is overwhelmed by good things to do and learn to taking a drink from a fire hydrant. A little bit of water from a gentle fountain can go a long way, he says. But put your mouth in front of a flowing hydrant, and things can get dangerous. What could have brought refreshment can also bring injury.

I am one who is convinced that the relentless flow of information, religious stimulation, and opportunity coming at us is indeed like a hydrant under high pressure, and that it is having a subtle effect upon our inner spirits, or as I have called it in other places, our private worlds. If I am correct, we can expect at least two things to happen almost at once.

First, as our eyes are drawn more and more to the events and data of the public world (even the Christian public world, if you please), the private world, the heart, becomes increasingly starved for attention and inner maintenance. More time for activity means less time for devotion. Doing more *for* God may mean less time *with* God. Talking becomes an effective substitute for meditating or listening. After all, something says to us, doing all these noble things isn't all bad. No, it may be good; but it may not always be best.

Second, and happening simultaneously, the busyness of our lifestyles is expending what passion we already have. In other words there is *output but no input!* And then there comes the inevitable moment when we become aware—like my friend of the last chapter—that we are going through motions, responding to habits. But the busyness is passionless. We are doing more and enjoying it less.

Let me propose that we need to understand what is happening to us as modern, Western Christians. Why are we telling one another with increasing repetition that we're tired and burned out? What is this frantic lifestyle doing to us? Shouldn't we occasionally cry *Stop!* and ask if this is the way Christ meant for us to live?

"But wasn't Christ always busy? Didn't He live a fairly pressurized life?" someone asks. "I don't see Jesus taking an evening off, playing miniature golf, scheduling four-week vacations. And when did Paul play? And where do you get any biblical basis for putting limits on the things we should be into? I don't see that as helpful to us when we are trying to get people to be more committed to the Christian mission."

"You may have a good point until you think again about Jesus' lifestyle in the biblical context, not in twentieth-century terms," I respond. "For example, when He went from town to town with His disciples, He moved on foot (or in a boat). There were long hours of quietness in the countryside on those walks. It wasn't the frantic jetting around—breakfast in Jerusalem, lunch in Damascus, and supper in Antioch." As J. B. Phillips put it:

It is refreshing and salutary, to study the poise and quietness of Christ. His task and responsibility might well have driven a man out of his mind. But He was never in a hurry, never impressed by numbers, never a slave of the clock. He was acting, He said, as He observed God to act—never in a hurry (Phillips, *Your God Is Too Small*, p. 56).

And that is important to remember. The fact is that the pace of life in Jesus' time was automatically governed not by inner discipline but by practical obstacles we have overcome by high-speed transportation, telephone, and organizational technique. But those obstacles guaranteed a more serene schedule.

If there were spaces in our calendars created by a slow-paced life, then we would not need to talk about artificial means of recreation, quietness, and renewal. We would know something of genuine tiredness at the end of an honest day's labor. We would not be talking about exhaustion of spirit, the loss of spiritual passion. We would not be checking calendars looking for just one evening when we could spend time getting our minds and hearts back into order again.

My Grandfather MacDonald traveled to Eastern Europe almost every year in the 1920s and 30s to preach and visit missionaries. After the war he resumed his annual schedule. And when he visited the continent, he would travel by steamship. When he arrived in France, he was refreshed by the several days of sailing when he had had the time to relax, read, study, and prepare sermons. The obstacle of the ocean and the slowness of the ship guaranteed the opportunity for the gathering, or the restoration, of his spiritual passion. And when he disembarked, he landed running!

It's different today in my generation. I would think nothing of flying to Europe and trying to engage in ministry within an hour of my arrival. And, most likely, my hosts would keep me as busy as possible since they would want to use every minute of my availability to justify the cost of the plane ticket. And I wonder why I fall into the weariness created by jet lag.

I suspect that Christ knew nothing of jet lag. Neither did my grandfather. Jesus was also not victimized by jangling telephones, filled mailboxes, international consultations, and Sunday school picnics.

Think with me a bit about weariness. It is not the honest tiredness of the body we will all feel at the end of a good working day. Rather it is the weariness of a tired spirit, the state of passionlessness where serving the Lord has become a tasteless experience, where the power and the delight of being a man or woman of God is missing. Where does that kind of spiritual dullness come from? And what are the consequences? And what, if anything, can we do to handle it when it comes or even avoid it so it won't come?

We will discover—when we stop and think—that our sense of weariness is a tricky subject. For example, we can be genuinely tired from busyness and pressure and not actually know it because what we are doing is so exciting and challenging that we lose ourselves in the sheer joy of it and refuse to hear the signals of fatigue. And, for a while, our bodies and minds will cooperate with us and permit us the extra exertion. That's life fueled by spiritual passion.

On other occasions we can think that we are tired, but we actually have much more energy in reserve than our bodies or minds will admit. But the task in which we are engaged is not attractive, and we may be afraid of failure. Now the body and mind protest, and they may signal exhaustion, a false kind. Why, for example, do I automatically grow drowsy the minute I try to pray? Why is it that I might feel an absence of energy the moment my wife suggests doing a task that will benefit a needy person?

Funny, these feelings of weariness. They are hard to depend upon, unless you figure them out.

When I was an athlete on the track and cross-country course, my teammates and I thought about this sort of thing. We studied weariness, its origins and effects. We learned to discriminate between *feelings* of fatigue and *genuine* fatigue. This was important because the challenge in running is as much mental conditioning as it is physical conditioning and development of brute strength. Most of the tiredness I experienced at the midpoint of a competitive

31

run was in the mind, not in the legs. It was helpful to know that. There is a passion of sorts in running, and you can't win a big race without it. The passion is cultivated and has to be maintained. Fatigue is the enemy of the runner's passion, and fatigue is the result when the passion is gone.

Therefore, I learned to analyze my weariness in the midst of competition and to pose the question, *Where is this fatigue I feel coming from?* More than once I had to ask myself in the third mile of a five-mile run, *Why do I want to stop running right now, quit this race—even the team—and go home to a comfortable bed like any other sane person? Are these signals I'm getting from my body real or false?*

These are not unlike the sorts of questions a man or woman in Christian responsibility ought to ask. *What is it that I feel? And where are the feelings coming from? Are they real? What are they telling me?*

Study the life of Christ, and you will discover that He was never on the verge of passionlessness. He obviously understood how one gets into that kind of situation. It is no accident that before and after heavy periods of activity He went apart and stored up, or replenished, the inner energy or passion necessary to carry out His mission. And, again, it is no accident that He never seems to have engaged in activity that was beyond His reasonable limits. He was pulled or guided by a mission—"to seek and to save the lost" (Luke 19:10 RSV)—, but He also seemed to have had an inner governor that effectively checked any urge to do more than was wise and prudent.

It occurs to me that Christ would have been comfortable with the words of John Wesley, "Though I am always in haste, I am never in a hurry because I never undertake more work than I can go through with calmness of spirit."

Calmness of spirit is the necessary condition for a well-ordered life. How might such a calmness be ours? There are of course lots of answers to that question. But I'm convinced that the first answers come in understanding something about the origins of weariness. Let me trace these origins for you in the next chapters.

3

It's All Over!

Let's return to the world of running. Those who compete in the Boston Marathon are well acquainted with Heartbreak Hill, a slow and long, tortuous climb through the streets of Newton, Massachusettes, about two-thirds of the way into the twenty-six–mile race. It is at old Heartbreak that the best runners break from the pack and prove their superiority.

Smart competitors mentally plan for Heartbreak Hill. They know what the mind will tell them at that point in the run, and they stride through the first seventeen miles with that fact in mind. What they have done is to reserve a kind of mental energy, a passion you could say, because they know where the inner battle will be. That's what I mean, in part, when I say that runners study the issue of fatigue.

The Boston runners taught me something about spiritual passion. A wise person, I saw, knows how to look ahead and spot the places where fatigue, the loss of spiritual passion, is likely to happen and why. That person knows, therefore, how to gather the necessary energy or passion ahead of time, how to parcel it out during the most challenging periods, and *how to renew that inner force later on.*

Jesus, greeting His disciples back from their two-by-two

mission said, "Let's get away from the crowds for a while and rest" (Mark 6:31 TLB). He knew what kind of shape they'd be in. And so He arranged that boat trip to the countryside where they could be alone. When they got there, they were met by 5,000 people; it was hardly a place to recover one's passion. But the record would seem to suggest that He engaged the crowds while the disciples took most of the day off. You could say they were renewing their spiritual passion.

Interesting it is, however, that even when Jesus called upon them to aid Him in feeding the crowd, they were disinterested and discouraged about the possibilities. They had just returned from a missionary-like experience where they were able to report remarkable happenings that were obviously miraculous, and they could not handle one more simple challenge. "Send the crowd away" (Luke 9:12 RSV), was their only response. Is there an indication here of their loss of inner energy, their fatigued condition?

Yesterday's spiritual passion cannot be today's inner energy. Passion quickly dissipates; it must be renewed. Like the manna God gave the Israelites in the desert, spiritual passion spoils quickly. As Moses and his people had to collect manna daily, so must we restore spiritual passion regularly. We would be wise to know how it so quickly disappears and what we can do when that happens.

As I once learned to study fatigue and loss of courage in the pursuit of athletic excellence, so I have learned to study fatigue and loss of courage in the pursuit of Christian commitment.

It has been helpful to me, first of all, to realize that there are *conditions* of life that affect spiritual passion, conditions like the advisories the weather people put out for sailors,

35

stockmen, and travelers when the elements are turning hostile. So there are conditions when you and I can expect trouble ahead.

Some of these conditions are predictable; others are not. But I have lived long enough now to categorize them for myself, and in the majority of cases I am now capable of looking at events and situations around me and—like the runner at Heartbreak Hill—saying to myself, "No wonder I feel this way; look at what's going on."

When a young pastor, I had a dream to visit the people of my congregation at their places of work. They regularly saw me at my worksite when I was at *my* best; why should I not see them at the point of labor where they were at their best? I strongly believed in this process and began to carry it out.

I visited managers at their offices. I rode with salesmen on their routes. I saw people in manufacturing plants, labs, and stores. The word got around that I was serious about visiting such places.

"Come out to my job," a construction steelworker said to me. And I enthusiastically responded, "Only if you'll take me right up to the top of the building where you work."

"I'll do it," he said.

Three days later I found myself hard-hatted and ascending a ladder (straight up) to the fourth story of a steel skeletal structure. By the second story I was terrified, a surprise since I'd not known that heights could be a problem for me. But the "man" in me was not going to admit to fear. By the third floor I was holding on to each rung of the ladder with extreme care. When I reached the top of the ladder, my friend was standing ten feet away on a steel beam that *seemed* no wider than a clothesline.

"Come out here," he said grinning at my discomfort. And I inched myself along the beam like a first-time horse-

36

back rider. That day I lost my passion for visiting *every* man and woman at their jobs and trying to pretend that I could go wherever they went. I discovered conditions where one's inner resolve disappears and may never return. It took me some time before I was ready to say again, "I'll go anywhere you're doing your thing."

The boxer Sugar Ray Leonard, who retired after an eye injury, attempted a comeback and was knocked flat in the sixth round by a lesser opponent. The newspapers printed a photo of him sitting bewildered on the canvas. "What were you thinking at that moment?" a reporter asked.

"I was saying to myself, *It's all over,*" he answered. It was a dramatic picture symbolizing a condition where the passion to come back suddenly disappeared.

SEVEN CONDITIONS THAT THREATEN SPIRITUAL PASSION

When I ponder the varieties of conditions that threaten our passion to know and serve our God, I come up with seven different ones. They are helpful to know and describe because I then can spot the times they are most likely to occur and know how I should perform when they do. Let's start with one of the most obvious of the passion-threatening conditions.

1. The Drained Condition

Thankfully, I have never experienced the state of drunkenness in my life, but I do understand hangovers. And so does everyone who has ever engaged in substantial spiritual leadership.

Hangovers—of the type I am describing—often happen

37

on a Monday morning for a preacher or for others at the conclusion of any sustained period of time when there has been a lavish expenditure of inner resources. This is not a religious phenomenon by any means. Any person who is heavily involved with people in highly stressful encounters of problem solving, conflict, or sales will understand what it means to be drained.

As I have already emphasized, the supply of the energy, or passion, within the inner spirit is not inexhaustible; it can and will be depleted.

Young men and women tend *not* to know that. They surmise that the brute strength of their physical energy level can carry them on indefinitely. It can work for a while. But not forever! One day, having ignored this possibility, they awake to the extreme inner stress of exhaustion of spirit. It is a terribly confusing experience.

No description of the drained condition, which I call the hangover, can improve upon the account of the prophet Elijah. When Elijah hit bottom in his own spirit and fled to the wilderness, he determined that death would be preferable to the way he felt. How did the man get that way?

The desert depression was preceded by the Mount Carmel triumph. Elijah had been on the mountain three days earlier, engaged in a remarkable confrontation with the pagan priests of Baal who had been religiously captivating the people of Israel.

The sitting king and queen of the day Ahab and Jezebel were to blame for the ascendancy of the Baal priests, and, as a result, God had judged the land with a "no-rain" edict for three years.

Now the showdown had begun. Elijah had challenged the priests to a duel of sorts, and he had scored a spectacular victory by the end of the day. An altar had been erected on

38

the mountaintop. Two bulls were prepared for sacrifice: one for the Baal folk, one for Elijah. A vast crowd of countrymen had gathered to watch. Reputations were at stake. Elijah was very much alone; the priests had an army of supporters.

"You call on the name of your god and I will call on the name of the Lord; and the God who answers by fire, he is God" (1 Kings 18:24 RSV). It was a fairly straightforward process. Take your best shot, go first, shout loud. And they had.

All morning there had been the absurd scene of sincere, grown men dancing, screaming, cutting themselves in order to gain the attention of their god. And nothing had worked! ". . . they raved on . . . but there was no voice; no one answered, no one heeded" (1 Kings 18:29 RSV).

Finally, it was Elijah's turn. He repaired the long-ignored altar of the Lord, set wood and the prepared animal in place, and then—just to add drama to the situation—drenched the entire piece with water. Finally he prayed, "Let it be known . . . that thou art God in Israel, and that I am thy servant, and that I have done all these things at thy word. Answer me, O Lord . . ." (1 Kings 18:36–37 RSV).

Talk about passion! One man against a spiritually depraved nation, a powerful king and queen, and several hundred priests who by their numbers alone had to be intimidating. I've always considered this one of the great moments in biblical history.

God answered the prayer—with force! Fire flew from heaven; the sacrifice was consumed, and the flippant nation of Israel burst into applause—for the moment. It was an exceptional display of heaven's power in collusion with a faithful man who was angry and passionate about the spiritual corruption in his world.

But a few days later, there was this inevitable hangover. It is difficult to describe what the encounter on the mountain top must have taken out of Elijah. All we have is the record of his foul mood there in the desert. Having descended from the mountain, Elijah had received death threats from the queen, Jezebel, who was not a little embarrassed over the humiliation handed to her team of Baal priests. Her best response for the moment could only come in the form of empty words: We're coming after you.

> Then he was afraid, and he arose and went for his life and . . . he himself went a day's journey into the wilderness . . . and he asked that he might die, saying, "It is enough; now, O LORD, take away my life . . ." (1 Kings 19:3–4 RSV).

One might wonder why the man didn't send a message back to the palace, saying "Stick and stones may break my bones, but names will never hurt me." But Elijah was, by this time, wearied enough that he believed the queen's words and, having lost perspective, he fled the country to the desert. Was this the same man who performed on Mount Carmel? Yes, *and he was drained!* Even if it is at Elijah's expense, we should take great comfort and warning from his misery.

Take a hard look at Elijah under the broom tree, asking God that he might die. "It is enough; now, O LORD, take away my life; for I am no better than my fathers" (1 Kings 19:4 RSV). More than anything else, Elijah needed some sleep and some good food, and it was provided. "Arise and eat," an angel told him when he awoke, "else the journey will be too great for you" (1 Kings 19:7 RSV). And although that was not the end of the story, it put the prophet into something of a better mental condition to get on with the restoration of his spiritual passion.

Again, Elijah was simply drained. He had given out everything on the mountain top; nothing was left. Who is there that hasn't had the same experience?

Pastors or Christian workers whose peak days are Sundays awaken on Mondays wondering why they feel so empty. Some of my former partners in ministry used to have a private scheme of measurement by which we gauged our spiritual condition on Monday mornings. Seizing the old phrase "I feel as if a truck ran over me," we often asked one another, "But how many trucks?" Using a scale of one to ten, we considered a one-truck Sunday to be unusually mild while a ten-truck Sunday described the ultimate debacle that might create the need a week's vacation.

All of us with leadership responsibility, however, will have our version of a pastor's Monday morning. The simple explanation? You can't do work of a spiritual nature without energy going out of you. Jesus felt it acutely when a sick woman reached out and touched the bottom of His robe. "Someone . . . touched me," he said, "for I felt healing power go out from me" (Luke 8:46 TLB).

Individuals in a drained condition feel caught up in a sea of feelings that often runs counter to all the facts. There are strong senses of self-doubt and negativism. The mind seeks out all the possible minor (and major) errors that might have been made in the past hours, and then it amplifies them until all positive contributions are mentally blotted out. Drained people become supercritical of self and, of course, of others. They are convinced they have made fools of themselves, that nothing done or said will be remembered or implemented.

When men and women are drained, they often generate

41

moods that lead to their wanting to quit the tasks they've wanted to do the most. Like Elijah, they are convinced that their usefulness is over, that they are powerless to go any further.

General William Booth, founder of the Salvation Army, came to the point of feeling drained more than once. Once in such a condition, lonely and exhausted while on an extensive traveling itinerary, he was ready to throw his ministry over. Writing to his wife, Catherine, he said:

> I wonder whether I could not get something to do in London of some kind, some secretaryship or something respectable that would keep us going. I know how difficult things are to obtain without friends or influence, as I am fixed. But we must hope against hope, I suppose. (Begbie, *The Life of General Wm. Booth*, p. 422).

Pondering those words—and knowing exactly how the general felt—I realize that most people, then and now, visualized Booth as indestructible, resolved and committed no matter what, a giant of a man of God who could do anything his spirit and passion determined had to be done. Yet here, behind the scenes where no one can see, is the picture of an empty man who, like the boxer knocked flat on the canvas, seems to be saying, "It's all over."

To those of us who have ever worked with university students, the name of Howard Guinness is a special one. More than fifty years ago, Guinness, a young medical doctor, interrupted his career to tour the countries of the British Commonwealth, speaking to student groups and starting Christian student works in scores of colleges and universities. It was an exhausting routine, and Guinness was often drained. He described one moment:

Toward the end of the itinerary I was so tired that when I arrived back in Auckland [New Zealand] and was giving my report of the tour to a public meeting I had to stop and sit down without finishing. If I had said another word I would have found myself in tears. The nervous batteries had completely run down (Guinness, *Journey Among Students*, p. 71).

These drained moments can often be a time in which one feels a terrible sense of loneliness. Those of us who have traveled, giving talks or lectures, can attest to the sense of isolation in a hotel room after one has given out everything to a crowd of people for a day.

Some men will candidly share that in this lonely condition they are mysteriously drawn to sensual entertainment. Why? Simply, they are so drained of spiritual passion that they are open to anything that hints it might be able to renew the emptiness caused by giving out so much.

Knowing the drained condition so well myself, I long ago began to spot those times when I was most likely to face such an emotional and spiritual hangover. I knew of course that Monday was most likely to be a day like that, and I learned to spot periods of time on the calendar when there would be a heavy exhaustion of inner resources because of people contact, traveling, and intense problem solving.

It became important to schedule periods before and after when I could renew myself. And I learned to record the Elijah-like feelings in a journal or share them with my wife so that I could be more objective. And usually it works, but, of course, not always.

The *drained condition*—we ought not to be surprised when it hits us with force.

The runner at Heartbreak Hill in Newton isn't surprised.

43

He knows from experience and from the descriptions of others that he will feel exhausted and ready to quit as he plods along. But if he can make it through what he calls the physical and psychic wall, there will be better moments. If he doesn't quit now, there will be glory ahead. And he doesn't quit because he knows what weariness is all about and where it comes from. The passion to finish the course and to win remains.

4

Running on Empty

I have a childhood memory of my father habitually (or so it seemed to me) driving his car with the gas tank gauge always signaling EMPTY. Was it a subconscious game he played, a sort of gambling process that he secretly enjoyed?

"Dad, you're running on empty," we would say.

"I know," he would respond, "but when the needle gets to that point there's always a gallon or two left in the tank."

Perhaps my father was simply out of gas money and didn't want to admit it. I never found out. I just remember that there were too many worrisome journeys through places like the Holland Tunnel (in New York at rush hour) with the gas gauge silently screaming *the tank is dried out!* He never seemed perturbed by this.

Spiritually speaking, many followers of Christ run on empty most of the time and wonder why there seems to be no natural energy or passion to engage in spiritual life or work. And that highlights another condition of life in which spiritual passion is likely to be missing.

2. The Dried-Out Condition

The second condition of weariness can be described by

45

the phrase *dried out*. If the one who is drained has reached that state by exhausting resources, one who is *dried out* has reached that state by not taking anything into the inner chambers of life for quite some time. The two conditions are often closely associated.

The unfilled spiritual tank is an invitation to disaster, and many of us have known that awful moment when, like a car out of gas, we seem to cough and sputter and pull over to the shoulder, out of service, not able to go any farther.

We have all seen the car out of gas in a long tunnel or on a narrow bridge at rush hour. Thousands of people are potentially affected in the clogged-up mess that follows. And it can happen in spiritual life also. One empty spiritual tank can affect a score of other people. It's happened more than once.

Like many others, I am no stranger to the dried-out condition. This condition is often a danger for the multi-gifted person, one who has many differing gifts and capacities and who can appear to go for long periods, as they say, winging it.

Those with natural talents, like musicians, are quite vulnerable here. They can mistake the applause of the admiring crowds for God's blessing. Thinking that their ability to raise the emotions of people in an artistic setting is the same as being a tool in the hand of God, they begin to abandon any sense of need for spiritual passion or energy and move ahead on their own instincts. More often, what power they appear to have is sheer theatrics, not spiritual passion. Often the system seems to work for a long time, and then—disaster.

Some people are good with words, able to put concepts and stories together with ease. The words form into testimonies, Bible studies, sermons. Again, the crowd's response dulls the speakers into thinking that they are God's servants and that a schedule that leaves no time for the refueling of spiritual energy is justified by the apparent results—again, disaster.

How can one describe the dried-out condition? It is action without heart, oratory without power, doctrine without love. People who are dried out within can often be, for a while, the hardest workers. But they can also become the harshest critics and the most negative teammates.

Inside they experience a rising of turbulence—confused goals and motives and inconsistent, unexplainable patterns of personal performance.

W. E. Sangster describes the realities in his world when he concludes that he is spiritually dried out (P. Sangster, *Doctor Sangster*, p. 90):

I am a minister of God, and yet my private life is a failure in these ways:

a. I am irritable and easily put out.

b. I am impatient with my wife and children.

c. I am deceitful in that I often express private annoyance when a caller is announced and simulate pleasure when I actually greet them.

d. From an examination of my heart, I conclude that most of my study has been crudely ambitious: that I wanted degrees more than knowledge and praise rather than equipment for service.

e. Even in my preaching I fear that I am more often wondering what the people think of *me*, than what they think about my Lord and His word.

f. I have long felt in a vague way, that something was hindering the effectiveness of my ministry and I must conclude that the "something" is my failure in living the truly Christian life.

g. I am driven in pain to conclude that the girl who has lived as a maid in my house for more than three years has not felt drawn to the Christian life because of me.

h. I find slight envies in my heart at the greater success of other young ministers. I seem to match myself with them in thought and am vaguely jealous when they attract more notice than I do.

Again, people saw Sangster—as they would have seen General Booth—as a giant. But he alone knew when he was operating from a full heart or an empty one.

Is this not the condition of David when he faced the great dual temptation of adultery and murder? It is a dramatic example, but one can't read the story without realizing that the man was in the wrong place, doing wrong things when he got into personal trouble.

David should have been with his armies, doing what God had purposed him to do. He would have been stretched and pressed by circumstances, forced to seek spiritual guidance and direction. But he wasn't there! Rather, he was at home in a state of undeserved relaxation, with nothing to do and his spiritual disciplines laid aside.

What was the result? He was left with no passion to identify and stand against temptation, no passion to make him hungry for the guidance of God, no passion to produce a hunger to be strong, honorable, and effective as a man of God.

Dried out, David made a series of bad choices, and when he reached the bottom line of performance, he destroyed a number of lives. (One has the mental image of traffic stalled in a tunnel at rush hour because one person entered with an empty tank.) What's worse, it took David a year before he realized the full import of what he'd done.

When Nathan the prophet paid a visit to David, he had to resort to a parable to gain David's attention. Usually, parables are for people whose inner spirits are locked up, impervious to the Holy Spirit of God. It's clear that David was in rough shape spiritually when Nathan came to call. He was in no mood for getting right to the point. So, the parable, and it worked. David was (as they say) "had," shocked into the realization of his performance over the last year.

It must have been a terrible moment of self-realization as David came to grips with his own inconsistencies and hypocrisies. How, he must have wondered, could he have gotten himself into this sort of situation? Weren't the warnings abundant enough? How, after years of intimacy with God, could he have permitted himself to become so empty and resistant? I suspect David asked himself questions of that sort for the rest of his life.

I have known what it is to be dried out. On some occasions I have shared with younger men and women a bitter experience in my late twenties when I encountered the dried-out condition with force.

One Saturday morning I sat in our kitchen obviously rattled and withdrawn, and my wife, Gail, was trying to discern what it was that was bothering me. Suddenly, she asked one question too many, and I broke into weeping. Even now, I remember the next two hours vividly because it seemed as if I would never be able to stop the flow of tears.

Gail handled the situation with grace and strength. She permitted me to exhaust myself of tears and then began to quietly quiz me about the events that had led up to this strange experience.

For the previous two weeks I had minimized my sleep because of busyness; thus I was physically exhausted. I had allowed my schedule to become so packed that I had ignored any times of personal worship; thus I was spiritually empty. In what seemed to be a remarkable coincidence, I had presided at two funerals of indigent men who had died on the city streets and whose lives and deaths seemed to me to be so terribly meaningless. The experiences had profoundly affected me. Additionally, I had been reading a then well-known author who was launching an attack on matters of personal belief important to me, and I was not responding well to his logic.

On that Saturday morning I was a dried-out man. My resources were nonexistent. Years and accumulated experience later, I would know better than to get backed into such a corner. But I didn't know that then. It was a difficult way to learn an important lesson about being empty.

I can't help but wonder how many good men and women have utterly failed in a public sense because they began to operate on the treadmill of Christian leadership from a spiritually dehydrated condition. This dried-out, empty condition explains the passionlessness of many Christians more than anything else.

3. The Distorted Condition

Earl Palmer began one of his great books by providing a transcript of a radio commercial in the early 1940s:

According to a recent nationwide survey, more doctors smoke Camels than any other cirgarette. Three leading independent research organizations asked this question of 113,597 doctors: "What cigarette do you smoke, Doctor?"

The brand named most was Camel. Now you probably enjoy rich full flavor and cool mildness in a cigarette just as much as doctors do, and that's why if you're not a Camel smoker now, try a Camel on your T-zone, (that's T for taste and T for throat), your true proving ground for any cigarette. See if Camel's rich flavor of superbly blended choice tobaccos isn't extra delightful to your taste. See if Camel's cool mildness isn't in harmony with your throat. See if you too don't say, "Camels suit my T-zone to a tee" (Palmer, *Alive From the Center*, p. 14).

I was drawn to the commercial, first, because I remember it as a child, but, second, because I was impressed with how persuasive it must have been to people listening in those days. After all, these are doctors, experts, saying these things. If they smoke, why not me? Thousands of cases of cancer are the result of the so-called experts endorsing a product.

Spiritual passion is constantly under attack by the distortions of truth that pervade our times. We pass through a world in which there are, I am told, more than two thousand persuasion messages pressed at us each day. They come to us, for example, in advertising, direct human encounters, signs all about us (STOP HERE; NO FOOD OR DRINK ALLOWED; KEEP OFF GRASS), and endorsements by impressive people.

The mind filters out the large majority of these messages much like an executive secretary might sort the junk or the reroutable out of the boss's mail. We don't realize that some part of us is saying no all the time because the process is so automatic. What we are left with is a small set of decisions in response to a large number of messages—the supposedly major decisions that cannot be left up to our subconscious secretaries.

51

But even that small set of decisions is huge, and the decisions and choices we must make are wearisome. A newly returning missionary who had been in the two-thirds world* where one is fortunate to find any food at all in the stores told my wife of the shock of visiting an American supermarket upon her arrival back home.

"I was astonished to see the numbers of choices one had to make just walking the aisles of the market. Take the potato chip section. When I left the United States, there was one basic kind of potato chip. Now there are seventeen or more kinds: salted or unsalted, ribbed or unribbed, nacho, onion, barbecue, taco, sour cream and onion, and so on. Think of all the time and effort that has to be expended just to make these incredible numbers of choices between things in abundance."

Even though we are not aware of the relentless barrage of messages coming at us, the combined force of them is still doing a job on us. They quietly sandblast the soul, the seat of conviction and value, threatening our ability to make and implement priority decisions.

I cannot help but think of the Older Testament† character Lot as a man whose inner life became distorted by the realities about him. Always living off his uncle Abraham as a parasite, Lot had little inner defense when it came time to make a major decision regarding his destiny.

---

*This area has been called the third world for years. But more recently, internationals have been referring to the third world as the two-thirds world since the population and geography of the "third" world actually comprises two-thirds of the people and land mass.

†My choice of using *Older* is quite deliberate. Christians do the OT an injustice when they refer to it as merely *Old*.

The shared business of Abraham and Lot reached a point where it seemed best to split the assets and move in different directions. The supply of resources was inadequate for the flocks and herds they'd built up, and tension was increasing between their staffs. It's conceivable that the two of them had lost the sense of enjoyment in working together.

The magnanimous Abraham did not put the process of a division of assets and lands to negotiation. Rather he gave Lot the first choice to go in whatever direction he wanted. And Lot was only too willing to seize the advantage.

But he made his choice from a distorted perspective. "And Lot lifted up his eyes and saw . . ." (Genesis 13:10 RSV). Messages poured into his mind, suggesting that he should grab the green grass and the lush valleys to the south while they were available and as long as Abraham was "stupid" enough to give him a first shot at the property. And he listened to his eyes.

Malcolm Muggeridge is fond of quoting William Blake's poem (emphasis mine):

> This life's dim windows of the soul
> Distort the heavens from pole to pole
> And lead you to believe a lie
> When you see *with*, not *through*, the eye

Lot looked *with* his eyes and saw the beauty of Sodom. He did not look from an inner spirit of values and convictions that would have permitted him to see moral rot and filth.

What was not included in the headlines of the messages he received from the eyes was more or less in the fine print, only to be read later. The green valleys also included

Sodom and Gomorrah and the lifestyle that would ultimately cost Lot his family, his dignity, and any sense of credibility he'd ever enjoyed.

But another kind of distortion—not from the Sodoms of this world, but from the Jerusalems—may be observed. I would be suggesting nothing novel if I observed that the person who walks in Christian leadership is always in danger of a distortion of the spirit by negative outside influences that come from our world. But I might startle some if I were to suggest that distortion can come even from within the Christian community.

It has been my experience that one of the greatest enemies of my own inner well-being, my own spiritual passion, is the vast number of good experiences and opportunities available to me.

I have frequently found myself in the state of what I describe as oversensation. As one grows older, it is possible to be involved in so many interesting and exciting things that adrenaline becomes something of an addictive drug. Life becomes a peak-to-peak hopping of wonderful experiences, each a bit emotionally higher than the last until there comes a time when the peaks can't get any higher or more frequent.

The inner being is fed on thrills and excitements. It is a rather spiritually-deficient diet that leaves one exhausted and weary.

Does not all of this simply enforce the importance of maintaining an independent base of judgment about the messages coming our way? Whether the signals come from a world whose motives and methods are predominantly evil or from a world whose methods and motives appear to be biblically oriented, the danger may be the same. It is weariness, loss of spiritual passion: a dried-out tank that offers no energy to get where one has to go tomorrow.

I have memories of anxieties when my father headed across the George Washington Bridge with the needle on E. But the worse memories are those times when I suddenly felt needed by someone and sensed that within me there was nothing to give. My tank was empty. There was no passion from which to operate.

5

Further Threats to Spiritual Passion

On our first visit to Africa, my wife and I visited a tiny, up-country village in the Ivory Coast called Sepikaha where we met Chloe, a blind evangelist. That day the man had walked several dozen miles from his own village to get to Sepikaha where he preached regularly to a small group of Christians. We watched him in action, breathless with admiration for his courage to preach in a town where the religion of Islam was militantly practiced.

A few months after we had met Chloe, he was attacked and severely beaten by those who resisted his presence in Sepikaha. His blindness gave him no opportunity for defense. Yet when he had recovered from his wounds, he went back.

I have often pondered over the extent of the spiritual passion which repeatedly drove that man to walk those miles to villages like Sepikaha, preach to people he could not see, and keep on doing it after he came within an inch of losing his life. The beating had not destroyed his passion.

Paul knew those sorts of moments only too well. And there are indications that his own passion may have been threatened at one time or another.

A weariness is expressed in his words to the Corinthians,

"We do not want you to be ignorant of the affliction we experienced in Asia; for we were so utterly, unbearably crushed that we despaired of life itself. Why, we felt that we had received the sentence of death" (2 Cor. 1:8–9 RSV). I call this the devastated condition.

4. The Devastated Condition

The devastated condition is the fatigue that originates with people and events vigorously opposed to what one stands for. I hear Paul saying that there was a time when the opposition almost got to him, that the beatings, the imprisonments, the incidents of ridicule and outright persecution began to wear him down. I hear the old apostle hinting that there was at least one time when he was so tired of it all that he wished he were dead.

We cannot afford to take this Pauline self-disclosure lightly. All too often we have been provided models of the great saints that suggest they never grew tired or disheartened. Here is one of many occasions when Paul was consummately weary, weary enough to want to run from everything, even into the arms of death.

The Greek scholar R. C. H. Lenski pointed out that the word *affliction*, as Paul used it, describes a sense of pressure so intense "that we became weighted down exceedingly beyond ability so that we got to despair even of living on" (Lenski, *Interpretation*, p. 826).

Weariness sets in with conditions such as these. One can go for just so long in the face of outright opposition from people and events, and then there is a slow crumbling of resolve or resistance.

Paul was not specific about the events, and no one really knows why. Perhaps he didn't feel it necessary to be graphic, but he did want the Corinthians to know that he had passed through a numbing experience of inner pain. A lesser person than Paul would have caved in. That Paul did not is a testimony to his ability to renew his spiritual passion.

We do ourselves a serious disservice if we do not face up to Paul's feeling of devastation. We have wrongly read the heroes of faith if we assume that they never had Pauline moments of despair, if we suspect that our moments of hurt and heartsickness are unique and merely an indication of our spiritual immaturity.

David had such a terrible moment in his relationship with his son, Absalom. To a considerable extent he had himself to blame when Absalom "stole the hearts of the men of Israel" (2 Sam. 15:6 RSV) and created conditions under which David had to leave his beloved city of Jerusalem. The writer of 2 Samuel told the sad story of David's evacuation from his home, his throne, his palace near the worship center of Israel, and then from the city he'd built. To compound the insult, David was attacked, stoned, and cursed by an outraged distant relative of the late Saul, David's predecessor on the throne. Which hurt worse—the stones or the verbal indignities—is hard to tell. But the journey to a safe place out in the eastern deserts must have been a devastating experience.

When the trip came to a conclusion in the eastern wilderness, the writer said, "The King and all his men were worn out when they reached the Jordan, and there they rested" (2 Sam. 16:14 TEV).

It is the story of devastation, a man stripped of everything by his enemies. He is the epitome of weariness. How will he act in this terrible situation?

People pass through these sorts of situations all the time. Some fall apart; others gather strength and discover passion within that they never knew possible.

Wayne Alderson, known for his great Value of the Person movement, faced a devastating moment in his career as a steel executive. R. C. Sproul tells the story in his book *Stronger Than Steel.*

Alderson had stepped into a volatile labor situation at Pittron Steel and had initiated a process of labor relations that was unprecedented. Within a short time, the working conditions at Pittron began to change, morale increased, and so did worker productivity. Alderson had begun to prove that you can treat employees with dignity and respect and, as a result, produce a working environment in which everyone wins.

Ironically, Alderson's contribution became his own downfall. Pittron became an attractive acquisition for a larger company, and before long the Bucyrus-Erie Corporation consummated a deal to take over Pittron.

Sproul described the dramatic meeting between Alderson, who was manager of the acquired company, and the man who was chairman of the acquiring company when Alderson was informed that his concept of labor relations was incompatible with Bucyrus-Erie's policies. He must abandon his relations with labor or get out. The choice was his.

> Wayne's lips began to form an answer. His mouth was open, ready to say "yes," but what came out was "No sir, I will not give it up."

He was fired! Everything he had worked for was suddenly gone.

Wayne tried to imagine what it would be like to be unemployed. He was now a statistic, a casualty of the corporate wars. But he was not overcome with gloom. His spirits were lifted by the realization that the decision he had been so frightened to make was now behind him. The moment had come and gone; it had seemed almost easy. . . . Wayne was left to face the public's reaction to his firing. Alderson's public image was crumbling. Wayne was crushed with disappointment, but he felt no shame (Sproul, *Stronger Than Steel*, pp. 124–25).

We ought not to be surprised when the devastating moments come, when all outside supports are stripped away. It can be a time when passion is tested and sometimes sucked away. But for the person who knows how to renew and maintain spiritual passion, it can be a moment for great performance.

5. The Disillusioned Condition

Spiritual passion can also be neutralized in disillusionment: the deflation of great dreams.

"My husband's a dreamer," I heard my wife tell some people, "and most of his dreams are very, very expensive." I guess she's right. And being the dreamer that I am, I'm also aware that dreaming cost more than money. It often costs a sense of loss, those extreme moments of disappointment when something you want very, very badly doesn't happen.

You want to see people get behind a program, and they won't. You believe in a sense of direction for an organization, and the people won't provide the support for both good and bad reasons. You invest great personal energy in individuals in whom you see potential, and they fail at a key moment.

60

Disillusionment is such a painful experience for many of us. We are tempted to withdraw, to pledge that we shall never again dream.

The moments of dream deflation leave large marks upon the soul. It would not take me long to list most of the occasions when I thought I had had given birth to a great idea only to have it torn apart by those who were more interested in status quo, or proper procedures, or politics, or their own positions of security or recognition. Of course there were not a few moments when my dreams were just plain ridiculous, and someone had to tell me so.

But, nevertheless, each time a dream is deflated for whatever reason, it hurts badly. In my younger years the reaction was often emotional, and the usual temptation was to stop dreaming altogether. Spiritual passion dissolved, and for a while there was no fight left within.

Is Moses a picture of disillusionment when, at the age of forty, he became aware of the oppressed condition of his people in Egypt and began to dream about their liberation? One day he saw an Egyptian fighting with a Hebrew. In a moment of outrage he stepped into the fracas like a would-be hero, killed the Egyptian, and buried him. The fledgling dream assumed reality.

Did Moses assume that the intervention would make him a hero with his people? If he did, the next day when he attempted to conciliate two Hebrews locked in conflict and they utterly rejected him, he must have been shocked. "Then Moses was afraid" (Exod. 2:14 TEV). In outright fear and disillusionment, having made himself so vulnerable and having taken such a risk, Moses fled town for the desert.

The biblical text is sparing in its description. We are left to fill in the blanks with our imagination, and that is not

61

hard to do. I think of Moses' feelings as he journeyed into unknown territory in the heaviness of the hour. Such dreams; such disaster.

It took *forty years* for Moses to regain his nerve, to recover any sense of passion. The text is usually interpreted to suggest that God had to wait forty years until Moses was ready to listen to a more proper way to achieve liberation. And perhaps the people themselves had to wait forty more years until they were desperate enough to follow the now-prepared Moses.

But when the man returned to the site of his earlier disillusionment, he was ready to perform—God's way. His passion was generated and channeled. We all know what happened.

Moses helps all of us to understand that spiritual passion can be jeopardized when dreams and visions are dashed.

6. The Defeated Condition

There is a weariness that comes from total personal defeat. Perhaps this is the most common of all the varieties of weariness.

Who does not know the taste of failure? One suddenly feels utterly impotent, unable to live up to the set standards of faith. Or promises or commitments have been made, but then broken. Or disciplines and goals have been enthusiastically determined, and then abandoned.

Those in leadership have an obligation to their families, or the church, or the business to live at a higher quality level as models. And then comes the terrible moment of embarrassment when the model falls apart.

Peter is a model for us to consult. He was the great man of words, especially enthusiastic ones. His promise to Jesus to follow and die, if necessary, was an empty one. "I'm ready to go to prison with you and to die with you" (Luke 22:33 TEV). The promise may have been sincere, an expression of his deep affection for the Lord perhaps, but we soon discover that it was an unworkable promise.

Within hours Peter was a failure. And the failure wasn't achieved in a quiet, out-of-the-spotlight place. The promise began to unravel in the garden when Peter couldn't keep awake to pray. His failure snowballed when he stood by the Lord in the garden in the presence of the temple guard and drew a sword, the very thing Jesus had been saying wasn't a response to trouble. And it peaked with his several denials in the court of the high priest. And what made the defeat so humiliating was that the denials were not made in the presence of great and powerful figures, but rather in the company of peasants and servants, young people from whom Peter presumably had nothing to fear.

Luke describes the ultimate moment of failure by commenting that the rooster crowed just as the Lord had predicted and that Jesus—from wherever He was in the court—turned and looked at Peter. Peter must have felt that look like one feels the effect of a laser beam. "And he went out and wept bitterly" (Luke 22:62 RSV).

Passion does not dwell in the heart of the defeated. And Peter is a most graphic picture of a man who thought he was moving on passion and wasn't. And when he was defeated, all he could do was weep intensely and futilely. And for the next several days, Peter was a passionless man. The defeat was paralyzing.

7. The Disheartened Condition

Perhaps we can identify one more condition in which

passion is squelched. I refer to it as the disheartened condition. Another good word might be *intimidated*. We fall into the intimidated, or disheartened, condition when we begin to gain a view of people, events, or institutions that causes them to appear to be far more powerful than the God of our faith. And that's not hard to do.

The disciples illustrate intimidation, of course, when they were paralyzed by the coming of the temple guard in the Garden of Gethsemane and fearfully scrambled into the darkness. The spies sent into the Promised Land were, with the exception of Joshua and Caleb, intimidated by the power they saw, and they returned to Moses with reports of outsized giants and fortresses and led people to believe that they had gone about as far as they could go.

There is the fascinating description of Ahaz, an intimidated king of Judah, who lost his grip on God's promise that his throne was under divine protection. Refusing to relax in that assurance, he assessed the power of the enemies marching on his capital, and his heart "shook as the trees of the forest shake before the wind" (Isa. 7:2 RSV).

How much in contrast to him is the posture of Isaiah, the prophet delegated to bring Judah reassurance. Isaiah had spiritual passion. Why wasn't Isaiah intimidated? His answer was:

> The LORD spoke thus to me with his strong hand upon me, and warned me not to walk in the way of this people, saying: "Do not call conspiracy all that this people call conspiracy, and do not fear what they fear, nor be in dread. But the LORD of hosts, him you shall regard as holy; let him be your fear, and let him be your dread" (Isa. 8:11–13 RSV).

I have felt the feelings of intimidation as I have driven Storrow Drive into Boston. To the left as one drives along the Charles River are the beautiful buildings of Harvard, and to the right are the more austere dwelling places of the Harvard Business School.

Further down Storrow Drive, again to the left, is the campus of the Massachusetts Institute of Technology (MIT), many of the buildings roofed with antennas, satellite dishes, and other strange looking objects that suggest to the uninitiated that mysterious things go on there, that people are talking to the stars. Ahead are the buildings of Boston's downtown where many multinational corporations have their headquarters.

It is a temptation to allow all of that to rebalance the mind and spirit, to permit oneself to think that in places such as these offices, labs, and classrooms the real power to change and control history is being generated and discharged.

Spiritual passion can quickly dissipate when one compares these concrete symbols of human power to the abstract gospel of Jesus Christ, and it is tempting to say with the disciple who was disheartened over the inadequacy of the lunch to feed thousands, "But what is this gospel among so many?"

Langdon Gilkey's book *Shantung Compound* illustrates the issue powerfully. During World War II, a couple of thousand Westerners were impressed into concentration-camp-like quarters by the Japanese in North China. *Shantung Compound* is the story of how those people forged a community and shared life.

Gilkey, at the time a young optimistic professor, began his account of the camp's life by expressing awe over the knowledge and capacities of the people at Weihsien. As he participated in the attempts to organize the camp, he became persuaded that

The real issues of life are surely material and political: how we can eat and keep warm, be clothed and protected from the weather, and organize our common efforts. These matters are resolved by practical experience and by techniques, not by this or that philosophy or religious faith, however convincing an expression of that faith may be to the cool observer of the scene.

It was not that I thought religion wrong; I simply thought it irrelevant. What real function in actual life does it perform under conditions where basic problems are dealt with by techniques and organizational skill? I was quite willing to admit that there are people who are interested in the nature of man and the universe; and that apparently there are others who enjoy religion and going to church. But, unlike food and sanitation which one must have in order to live, is not religion merely a matter of personal taste, of temperament, essential only if someone wants it but useless if one does not happen to be the type that likes it? Is there any "secular" use for religion; does it have any value for the common life of mankind? (Gilkey, *Shantung Compound*, pp. 73–74)

Gilkey's questions bore into the spirit of the reader. They are intimidating questions, disheartening questions until answered. He is suggesting that the person of faith is wasting time in small, irrelevant things.

Wherever I turned, everything I saw reinforced this view. Of what use to our life were the vocations of teaching philosophy or preaching Christianity. Those of us who had performed these tasks in the outside world now carried our weight of camp work yes—but not in *those* roles. We were useful only insofar as teacher or evangelist became able stoker or competent baker.

66

Then he went on again:

> My feelings found full expression one Sunday when, rush-
> ing by the church bent on some errand for the Housing
> Committee, I heard a familiar hymn ringing out through
> the open windows. I asked myself irritably, "What for—
> when there are so many important things to be done?"
> And shaking my head in disbelieving wonder, I went on
> about my business (Gilkey, *Shantung Compound*, p. 75).

Not a few of us who have chosen to follow Jesus Christ
have listened to arguments like this. At times they have
seemed quite persuasive, enough to draw off our spiritual
passion and make us feel as if, in reality, we have nothing to
offer the real world. The temptation grows to think that the
fulcrum of history is not in the gospel of Christ but in the
visible power of business, politics, or force.

Gilkey's account of affairs at Weihsien concluded with a
strange and fascinating twist. The community, marvelously
organized with competent skills and expertise, began to
come apart. Graft, corruption, and open strife invaded
their community. The talented experts—who were able to
devise systems, machines, and organizations to solve practical problems—weren't able to provide an ongoing sense of
purpose for life, a moral imperative for people to serve one
another and strive for common benefit, a rule of life by
which people could maintain dignity and hope.

Gilkey had discovered what was the domain of those who
practiced their faith devoutly and practically.

> There was a quality seemingly unique to the missionary
> group, namely, naturally and without pretense to respond
> to a need which everyone else recognized only to turn

aside. Much of this went unnoticed, but our camp could scarcely have survived as well as it did without it. If there were any evidences of the grace of God observable on the surface of our camp existence, they were to be found here (Gilkey, *Shantung Compound*, p. 192).

As Gilkey became aware that there were deeper issues than expertise and power, so did I constantly learn to re-mind myself that the beautiful towers of Harvard and the antennas of MIT housed the best the human race can offer history. But it is still the power of Christ's gospel that gives meaning to history and provides an insight, as well as a way, to change the human heart. That assurance renews spir-itual passion.

I've outlined seven conditions in which spiritual passion is often threatened. There are many more, and perhaps among the seven there are many overlaps. It is difficult to grow or renew passion when one is living in one or more of these conditions. They create a weariness that saps every positive quality and energy we need to be effective followers of the Lord.

I have found it extremely helpful to deliberate over the existence of these various conditions. It is actually quite possible to predict when any of these conditions is ap-proaching; it is much like the symbols on a weather map that tell me a cold or a warm front is coming through. So I've learned to listen to the advisories and to brace myself. For people in whom the Holy Spirit is working, living without spiritual passion is intolerable. An awareness of the conditions that might make that happen is therefore indispensable.

6
Those Who Bring Joy

Our spiritual passion is affected by the conditions in and around us. But spiritual passion, or energy, is also affected by the people who populate our personal worlds.

Being with people is exhausting. Ask a mother who has spent the day with two small children. Talk to the businessperson who has spent the day negotiating budgets with department heads. Or get the opinion of a nurse who has spent the day at the bedside of a dying patient. At the end of a day they are spent, sometimes ready to run.

But they have just been talking, sitting and talking. Why, ask those who work with their hands, is that so tiring? It's tiring because people contribute to, or draw from, our inner energy levels in ways we are not even aware of. They tax our minds and our spirits, and the resulting fatigue can sometimes be worse than that after a day's work on a construction crew.

I can think of certain people in my world whose company invigorates me, and when they leave, I am full of resolve, ideas, and intentions about God, self-improvement, and service to others. I can also think of people in my world whose presence exhausts me. And when they leave, I am ready for a long, long nap.

An old friend of mine used to say of people, "Some folk bring joy wherever they go; others bring joy *when* they go." We need to understand the people of our world and how they play a part in the potential invigoration or weariness of our lives.

Understanding the effect people have upon us will help us to know where our spiritual energy goes and when we can anticipate that we will need to restore it.

In my earliest years of Christian ministry I was not smart enough to understand fully the dynamics of what was happening, but I was quite aware that the people around me on any given day had a significant effect upon my sense of faith and its vitality. As I've already observed, there were those who constantly caused me to reach for higher plateaus of growth, while there were others who left me, as it were, gasping for air. The former I pursued; the latter I fled.

But fleeing, of course, would not have been ministry. I understood that I had been called as a servant to the broken and the hurting, and somehow I was going to have to adjust to that and pay the necessary price.

But I did begin to discover that anyone in the role of a leader becomes a target for many kinds of people—those who want to use the leader as a point of influence for their particular cause or concern; those who want to be near the leader because they deem him or her to be the top of a social pyramid and, therefore, a guarantor of popularity; and those who gain attention by trying to get prominent people to focus upon their problems.

Naturally, I began to discover that there were other kinds of people in my world—those who would not intrude into my calendar unless invited but who always had a word of encouragement or sound counsel; those who came wanting to learn and ask solid questions; and, of course, those with genuine personal need who came seeking a prayer, a strong arm, a word of grace and hope.

You don't have to be the pastor of a large church or a well-known, successful person to face the onrush of people. Any person in any kind of leadership will discover that people work is a never-ending process. And when this process is not understood or carefully monitored, it can have adverse effects upon one's spiritual passion.

FIVE KINDS OF PEOPLE THAT AFFECT SPIRITUAL PASSION

For me, monitoring means measuring and categorizing. And you can do that even in people work. For example, I came to see that in my world there are five kinds of men and women with whom I must constantly deal. An overage of exposure to any one kind sets up imbalances.

1. The Very Resourceful People: They Ignite Our Passion

Let's call the first group the VRP's, the very resourceful people who *ignite* our passion. Of course my parents were my first set of VRP's when I was a child. But then others came along, and I have enjoyed a chain of VRP relationships ever since the age of eight.

VRP's are those who are sometimes called mentors, shapers of life. Some might even call them surrogate fathers and mothers. One is never sure when a VRP relationship begins; in most cases it just seems to happen naturally. I think it is a gift from God. The important thing about Christian VRP's is that they *ignite* our passion for faith and Christlike performance.

71

The first VRP I ever remember was a working associate of my father's. I was drawn to his presence as an eight-year-old boy because it was clear to me even in my childish perspective that he believed in me. I felt strangely adult in his presence, a sense of being accepted and appreciated.

Another VRP relationship came in the form of a married couple who invested themselves in young people of high school age. Their home was always open; their time was ours; they appreciated the perceived seriousness of our romantic or family problems and offered (when asked) possible solutions.

A third VRP was a track coach who set performance standards according to personal excellence. His was a relationship not only of encouragement but also of rebuke. One did not want to displease the coach. It wasn't that he showed anger; you simply became aware that he was less than pleased by what was happening, and one experience of that kind was more than enough. He knew how to persuade an athlete to accept a certain amount of pain in order to reach higher levels of potential, and he knew how to turn athletic performance (winning or losing) into a character-building moment.

Other VRP's included a college parachurch worker, a Presbyterian pastor and his wife, an older single man, a seminary president, and a church history professor. All these—and others, of course—played a unique role in shaping me. They rarely entered into my world that they did not provide a resource, a growth point. And they rarely left my world at the conclusion of an encounter that I did not feel lifted, impelled to greater growth, and more aware of both flaws and possibilities.

The fact that they always make a positive contribution to one's world is an important distinction about VRP's, and it sets them apart from some of the others I will be mentioning. When I engage in the monitoring and evaluation of relationships, I note these people as making a three-plus (+ + +) addition to who we are and what we are doing.

Now the temptation is to want to be with people like this all the time. But that could be as unhealthy in the long run as the decision to remain at home in a child-parent relationship for the rest of one's life. It is certainly a protective way to live, and it helps on the bills, but it would never foster the independent and resourceful spiritual passion we're talking about that makes one a force for faith.

To be with a certain number of VRP's is a necessity. We all need those whom we can look to in a moment of uncertainty. But to be with them all the time would be stifling and, eventually, passionless. Jesus understood this all too well and appreciated the fact that three years with the disciples as their VRP was all they needed.

"It is to your advantage that I go away," He said (John 16:7 RSV). They'd had enough; the in-dwelling Holy Spirit could take over now, He told them.

A highlight in Christian history is the work of the Clapham sect, a group of Christian laypersons who lived in nineteenth-century England and marked their generation through their efforts in government, business, and the arts to bring about social change and order in the name of Christ.

One biographer of William Wilberforce, a Clapham sect member, recorded the observation of a young person who watched the men and women of Clapham in their private lives:

These wise men never endeavored to mold our unformed opinions into any particular mold. Indeed it was needless

73

for them to preach to us. Their lives spoke far more plainly and convincingly than any words. We saw their patience, cheerfulness, generosity, wisdom and activity daily before us, and we knew and felt that all this was only a natural expression of hearts given to the service of God (Lean, *God's Politician*, p. 100).

This is a brilliant description of VRP's and their effect upon those around them. They are the kind who make a supreme contribution from which we ourselves draw. We study their ways and then customize them for ourselves. We lean upon them for direction and approval. We gain energy from their courage and maturity. They are in every sense of the word our resource, and from them we can draw our first senses of passion.

2. The Very Important People: They Share Our Passion

The second kind of person in our worlds is what I have often called the VIP's, the very important people who *share* our passion. These are my teammates, the men and women with whom I am most closely associated: fellow workers, close friends who share the workload to which we are all called, or those with whom we share a common affection.

Barnabas was VIP to Paul (although for a short while he may have been VRP); so were Silas and Luke. I suspect that Aquila and Priscilla would have to be included. Paul used a beautiful word about VIP's in Philippians, chapter 4 when he used the word *yokefellow* to refer to those who had shared the yoke of ministry together. Yokefellows are the VIP's, and most of us have been fortunate to have known a few of them.

74

VIP's also make a contribution, what I have called a two-plus (+ +) contribution. Are there problems and conflicts with them? Sooner or later. But minimally so, and not so that one dwells upon such experiences. When we are with VIP's, we are all aware that the challenges we face are bigger than we and that the genius of our relationship is in the fact that the whole is greater than the parts. With VIP's we do not spend large amounts of time trying to get along, or debating over whose philosophy will prevail, or determining who is in charge. We are bound together to get a task done, and get it done we will.

VIP's *share* our passion. Together we stir one another up and goad each other to better and more faithful performances. VIP's keep us looking at the right goals; they are not hoodwinked by excuses and rationalizations. They sense when we are hurting or when we are in need. They delight in our successes and weep with us when we are disappointed.

For some years I have been a student of Charles Simeon, a nineteenth-century Church of England pastor in Cambridge. In his younger years his mentor (his VRP) was Henry Venn. In a letter written to Venn in 1783 Simeon, spoke of a VIP friendship with John Riland who gave him sharp but useful criticism on a sermon he had just preached. This friendship was VIP-ship at its best.

What a blessing—an inestimable blessing is it to have a faithful friend! Satan is ready enough to point out whatever good we have; but it is only a faithful friend that will screen that from your sight, and show you your deficiencies. Our great apostasy seems to consist primarily in making a god of self; and he is the most valuable friend who will draw us most from self-seeking—self pleasing—and self-dependence, and help us to restore to God the authority we have robbed him of (Carvs, *Memories of the Life of Rev. Charles Simeon*, p. 32).

3. The Very Trainable People: They Catch Our Passion

If VRP's *ignite* our passion and VIP's *share* our passion, a third kind of person *catches* our passion. I call them the VTP's, the very trainable people. They are to us what we were to those whom I've called VRP's.

Now *we* are the ones who ignite passion; *they* catch it! Here, of course, we are looking at biblical relationships such as Paul and his relationship to Timothy, Eli to Samuel, and Elijah to Elisha.

We are watching Mordecai ignite passion in Esther (his niece?) when he challenges her by saying, "who knows whether you have not come to the kingdom for such a time as this?" (Esther 4:14 RSV). Those words more than anything else thrust her into action that eventuated in the saving of thousands of lives.

VTP's make a one-plus (+) contribution to our worlds. They usually give, seldom take. And although VTP's tax our strength, we are usually glad to cooperate because we sense the possibilities in them.

We draw them to our side and open our lives to them. In the very sharing of ourselves we stir our own passion to serve and grow because we see the immediate effect it has upon them.

The further we are along the passage through adulthood the more important it becomes to have about us a small collection of very trainable people. It has often been

76

pointed out that this is exactly what Paul is urging on Timothy when he wrote:

What you have heard from me [VRP] before many witnesses entrust to faithful men [VTP] who will be able to teach others also [more VTP] (2 Tim. 2:2 RSV).

I am of the conviction that after a person passes the fortieth year of life, the investment in VTP's should become an increasing priority. So that we may provide the possibility of a succeeding generation of leaders and godly men and women.

The VRP's, and VIP's, and the VTP's of our lives generally make a positive contribution to our passion. Having been with them, our goals and objectives are clearer than ever. Our desire to pursue higher levels of maturity and effectiveness will increase. Thank God for them. We couldn't make it without their part in our experience.

But there are some others whose contributions are far more taxing. They tax our spiritual passion, drastically.

7

The Happy and
the Hurting

Two other kinds of people in our worlds have an effect upon our spiritual passion, and they are hard to describe in enthusiastic terms. But they are there and we must know who they are. These people crowd our horizon, seeking personal attention. And when they have gotten what they came for, we are tired people.

4. The Very Nice People:
They Enjoy Our Passion

I call the fourth group the VNP's, the very nice people who *enjoy* our passion. They come in large numbers, and we love to have them around.

VNP's clap and laugh and build our egos. They make people in public Christian leadership very happy because they fill pews and rooms and programs. En masse they provide substantial amounts of money (each giving a very small part) to fuel organizations sometimes called ministries.

VNP's are wonderful people; they are good people. And we make many fine friendships with VNP's. But the truth of the matter is that the overall contribution of the VNP is imperceptible. In contrast to the three-plus contribution of a VRP, the VNP has to be labeled a zero-plus contributor. They do not add to our passion; nor do they seriously diminish it. They simply enjoy it. Being around people who exude spiritual energy can be a pleasurable experience if one professes Christianity.

One is reminded of a childhood spoof on various breakfast cereals: they don't snap, crackle, and pop. They don't turn colors; they're not coated with sugar; and they're not shot from guns. What do they do? They simply lie in the bowl and sop up the milk. So is the role of the good old VNP who comes into our world often in large numbers.

Jesus never turned His back upon the VNP's in His world. He saw them as sheep without a shepherd, and He treated them with dignity and possibility. That's important to note, for from the midst of the VNP's there came certain folk who eventually became VTP's (each of the twelve was probably a VNP at first) and perhaps even later VIP's.

It is true, however, that when the crowds of VNP's got too large, the Lord would sharpen the blade of His teaching. He would make it clearer and clearer that there was a dramatic cost to discipleship. It was almost as if He were saying the size of this crowd suggests that you haven't heard me plainly enough or some of you wouldn't be here; so let me give it to you another way. And when He finished restating His message, many would then leave because they finally understood that no one can remain forever in the presence of Christ and be a VNP.

That is exactly what happened in John, chapter 6.

Many of his disciples, when they heard [his message], said, "This is a hard saying; who can listen to it?" But Jesus, knowing in himself that his disciples murmured at it, said to them . . . "there are some of you that do not

79

believe." For Jesus knew from the first who those were that did not believe, and who it was that would betray him. . . . After this many of his disciples drew back and no longer went about with him. Jesus said to the twelve, "Do you also wish to go away?" Simon Peter answered him, "Lord, to whom shall we go? You have the words of eternal life . . ." (John 6:60–61, 64, 66–68 RSV).

You can see the sorting process going on here. VNP's were welcomed into the presence of Christ, but only for a while. And then they had decisions to make.

My comments are not meant to ridicule the overwhelming numbers of people who crowd churches and religious gatherings. Rather they are meant to help us understand who the VNP's are and what effect they will have upon those of us who are in leadership and people development.

It is startling to realize that in church life most of our heavy expenditures are for the very nice people. VNP's fill the pews, the parking lots, and the classrooms and sop up the milk. We build and expand all too often for the convenience of the VNP's. VIP's and VTP's would normally accept great inconveniences in order to martial and redirect the material resources of the church into the world beyond: evangelism, mission, Christian service. But, unfortunately, VNP's, the large majority of congregations in the Western, unpersecuted world, prefer facilities, times, and programs built on personal convenience and comfort, and they are usually accommodated because the very magnitude of their numbers convinces leaders that the program is successful. This is disturbing to ponder.

Spiritual energy or passion is profoundly affected by the VNP's. In a sense, sopping up the milk means sopping up the passion. Leaders spend exorbitant amounts of time solving the problems of programming, interpersonal conflict, and enlargement that VNP's create by their presence. Laypeople and pastors who are responsible for the guidance and shepherding of VNP's know that in the best of all circumstances, the task is wearing and draining. Although the VNP's may swell the ego with their applause and conditional loyalty, they exhaust the spirit through their desire to take whatever the leader has to give.

When Gail and I were just beginning our ministry, we felt a desperate need to be liked and accepted by the people we had come to serve. Thus we responded to almost every overture for entertainment that came in our direction. It was a way—although quite a deficient way—of knowing that we were doing a good job, that we could make it in the pastoral lifestyle. We did not yet realize that sometimes people drew near to us because of the roles we were in, not because of the persons we were.

We were immediately courted by various groups who graciously invited us to their formal and informal gatherings. Some met monthly, others weekly. When we came, we were usually the center of attention because in the church social whirl our position as pastor and spouse put us—in human eyes—at the top.

We confused this sort of hospitality with an indication of people's spiritual commitment. And it was only after we had been with the congregation for a time that we began to discover that those who wanted our presence at all of their social activities were not always the people to be counted on when it came time to do the things we had come to the church to accomplish.

In this way we came to discover the existence of the VNP's. They were wonderful to be with, often encouraging with their compliments *and* gifts, but they were not always the team on the serving and the growing edge. It was hard to put distance between us and some of the activities of the VNP's. It had to be done wisely and discretely. They were enjoyable people, fun to be with. But we could not allow them to absorb all of our energy doing good things when the best things had to be done with the VTP's and the VIP's.

That was not an easy lesson to learn. And it still isn't!

5. The Very Draining People: They Sap Our Passion

A fifth and final group of people have a direct effect upon our spiritual passion. I have often quietly referred to them as the VDP's, the very draining people who *sap* our passion.

I do not wish to write of VDP's unkindly, but they exist in all of our worlds and must be carefully identified. Until we understand who they are and how they touch our lives, we will not fully understand why we experience weariness and passionlessness at times.

Very draining people affect our passion in just the way that their label suggests: they *drain* it. And they do so relentlessly. I am not trying to be uncharitable but merely factual when I suggest that their relationship to the leader is usually on the minus (−) side of the flow of energy.

I know that some will quickly wish to argue that there is a certain kind of energy that develops merely from the joy of serving the hurting and the lonely, and I would not want to argue with that. What I will want to point out, however, is that that sort of joy lasts only so long and then, in most cases, changes to a kind of exhaustion that must be addressed quickly or it will have ill effects.

In my early adult years when I was intent upon becoming the very best Christian leader I could, I responded as fully as I could to every person who crossed my path with any hint of need. Those who needed to visit with me immediately gained my attention. My phone was available for all callers, and I generally permitted them to control the length and pace of the conversation. Before and after any meeting in which I was a participant, I was ready to receive anyone who said I was needed.

I have memories of the man who had some serious personal struggles and found the supper hour a convenient time to call me nearly every evening. One member of a church board, who had a problem with virtually every issue we were facing, had to tell me in detail why he disagreed with each decision and why he had to take a stand against it. And a woman who had stumbled into a bad marriage (fifteen years ago) needed to report in full to me the evidence of that unfortunate relationship every Sunday after church.

Add to these an emotionally struggling young man in desperate need of attention from all authority figures, an adult woman who was always causing conflicts among Christians by her undisciplined tongue, and not a few people who were chronically sick and either needed comfort to deal with their aches and pains or explanations to understand why they were in these difficulties.

I discovered as time went by that every cluster of people (business, school, church) has a percentage of people who have to be labeled VDP's. And when that group is Christian in intention and orientation, its members try hard to care for and serve the VDP's. The good news is that this serving often pays off, and those who were draining actually become useful and trainable.

Then again, one can conceivably be a VDP to one person but not to another. For example, Paul considered John

Mark a VDP who could not be trusted for a second missionary journey, but fortunately, Barnabas saw John Mark's potential for a VTP or VIP and didn't agree with Paul's assessment.

I would type Judas Iscariot as a VDP among the disciples. He appears to have been a whiner, a constant critic, a hanger-on who contributed—as far as we can see—very little to the group.

Few people in the New Testament qualify for the VDP medal, probably because this section of the Bible is so centered on action people on the move. The obviously immoral church member at Corinth was a drain on the church's life, and Paul was disturbed that the people did not see that. Euodias and Syntyche were becoming drains upon the Philippian congregation by their inability to resolve their conflict. Paul wanted that conflict solved as soon as possible. He knew pending relational disaster when he saw it.

One does see some examples of VDP's in the Older Testament. There were times when Moses must have been tempted to think of the entire Hebrew nation as a drain on his leadership. Joshua would certainly suggest Achan as a draining person since his sin caused the defeat of the army at Ai. Nehemiah had a number of VDP's during his attempt to rebuild Jerusalem's walls. They were in and out of the camp: critics, slow movers, men with hidden agendas.

When God called Gideon to lead the people out from under the domination of their enemies (Judg. 6), He stripped all potential VDP's away in order to get the task completed. The inner drains were cleaned up in Gideon's own family life when he was commanded to destroy the pagan altars in his father's backyard before proceeding any further.

When Gideon massed his armies (over thirty thousand troops) to face the enemy, the first thing God called upon him to do was cut away those who were fearful and send them home (see Judg. 7:3). I've often wondered how Gideon took it when twenty-two thousand men walked away from that reverse invitation. But when it came time for action, there was no place for the VDP's.

We must not go a step further without recognizing that it is often from the ranks of the draining people that we begin ministry and lift people up to a position of growth and usefulness. So the long-term answer in any cluster of people is not to rid oneself of the draining people but rather to understand three important things about them and the groups of which they are a part.

First, VDP's will be drawn (like mosquitoes to blood) to any healthy group of people, and they will remain until they become self-sustaining or until they are pushed away.

Second, a healthy cluster of people will lose its vitality (its group passion) mysteriously and unpredictably because there are simply too many VDP's to sustain. The life of the group becomes problem- and crisis-oriented, and forward movement toward any kind of objective becomes impossible. Like a ship with dead engines, the crowd is dead in the water.

Third, VDP's who are permitted to relentlessly drain leaders of their passion will ultimately create a climate in which no one will want to serve in leadership capacities. Again and again, we have seen examples of young men and women who were ready to give maximum energy to the pursuit of some objective fade out because they were not protected from the VDP's.

I have great affection for certain brothers and sisters (VIP's) who understood this principle when I was the pastor of a large congregation. At the conclusion of worship services, they would come to my side and engage some of those who desired merely to gain my attention, not to call upon me for important pastoral issues. In private I called them my spiritual body guards. I think that I would not have survived if it hadn't been for them.

I was a number of years into my life as a pastor before I made a startling discovery. It was my calendar that taught me the hard lesson: the VNP's and the VDP's were accounting for the major percentage of my available time.

I was making a serious mistake. Because the *nice* people were so pleasant to be with, and because the *draining* people requested so much time, I had little prime time left over for the *resourceful* people, the *important* people, and the *trainable* people. None of these three made the demands upon me that the other two did. And I, because they made so few protests, left them alone as a rule because I thought I was where I was most needed. An error of great magnitude!

A check on the priorities of our Lord will show that He spent ample time with the *draining* and the *nice* people in His path: the sick, the anguished, the critic, the curious. But they never captured His full schedule. In fact they account for relatively little of it. Rather Christ appears to have maximized His time with the *resourceful*, in His case His heavenly Father. He reserved heavy time for the *important* and the *trainable*, for Him the disciples (the twelve, the seventy, and a few close friends).

That was an important discovery for me because I found that in giving my time to the VNP's and the VDP's, I was making a long-range error both for them and me. By being instantly available at all times for them, I was inadvertently teaching them an unhealthy dependence upon me as a leader; I was feeding their need to relate only to someone they conceived to be a special leader who, by his attention, provided them with a sense of importance that was neither authentic nor earned.

But even more significantly, by spending my prime time with these two groups, I was expending my own energy in nonrenewable ways. Every minute of that time was a one-way flow of passion (outward), sometimes necessary (as in the case of the woman who touched Jesus' robe) but, in the long run, seriously debilitating.

We grow weary when we do not learn this lesson in time. I have watched many laypeople quit responsibilities, even become embittered over church activity, because no one taught them how to protect themselves from draining people.

I do not want to be misinterpreted in my discussion of the VNP's or the VDP's. They are very much a part of the assembly of believers. And they must be ministered to. But we must understand that they will, by their very nature, make greater and greater demands until the healthy Christian's energy level has been dissipated to the point of exhaustion and weariness.

If we wonder why we are often weary, a look at the distribution of time on the calendar in past weeks may well provide the answer.

Time with the VRP's, the resourceful people of our worlds, will build our passion. Time with the VTP's, the trainable people, will tax us for sure, but it is eventually restorative because these sorts of people pick up our passion and our burden and move with us.

But if our calendars reveal that the predominant part of our time is merely with the nice and the draining, then we must not keep wondering why we lose our vitality. These people take but do not give, and unless we pause and re-balance, the result is often disaster.

Years ago my wife and I became acquainted with a young woman in our community. It soon became apparent to us that she was a problem drinker. The day came when it was necessary for her to face the situation, and the pain of coming to grips with her tendency toward alcoholism was for her and us unforgettable.

She was a classic example of the very draining person. The hours of conversation over the phone and in the home were incalculable. The temptation to write her off was great. More and more people entered the mix of caring for her, and when they were together, it was not unusual for the conversation to center on what to do for her.

We all loved this person very much, and we saw that she had large reservoirs of human potential if she could gain a hold over her addiction.

It took ten years! With the power of Christ, the love of people, and the resources of various organizations, the VDP we had known for so long became a VTP, and then a VIP. Today she is for many a VRP. Whenever I think of turning my back upon a VDP, I think twice because I see what she has become.

Nevertheless, I have learned that VDP's cost energy and passion, and that leaders who permit an imbalance of contact with these, the hurting people of our world, can expect to pay a massive bill in inner exhaustion.

The people around us give and they take. Whenever we are in public, we can expect that a flow of passion will be moving one direction or another: toward us or away from us. It's important to know that.

88

8

Friendly Fire

The monument to the Vietnam War dead in Washington, D.C., is a sobering site. Go there, and you are liable to come away with intense feelings and not a few tears. The architect seems to have understood the mixed passions surrounding that conflict.

Inscribed on the black granite walls are the names of more than thirty thousand men and women who died for their country. But somehow the honor reflected by the monument seems mixed with a sense of futility over the manner in which the war was conducted and the way it ended. Is the emotion one feels when standing before the monument a response to the bravery and sacrifice of the dead? Or is the emotion one feels a response to the waste of human life, given the tragic conclusion?

When the first U.S. military forces hit the beaches of Vietnam, Americans experienced a passion of sorts; as President Johnson announced the escalated military presence, Americans experienced a sense of optimism. Across America there was a general confidence that what we thought was a mess in Southeast Asia would quickly be cleaned up with a minimum of fuss or human loss. Most Americans—some outstanding exceptions, of course—felt confident of that! How complete was our misjudgment!

A few years and many frustrating battles later, the national confidence was shattered, and our young men and women came home, having neither won nor lost. They had been prepared to face concentrated armies on open fields of warfare, and they had been equipped with modern military weapons. But, unfortunately, there was rarely an open field of battle, and the enemy utilized strategies and weapons our troops had never seen before.

The war featured an almost invisible adversary, always there, yet seemingly impossible to locate in gun sights. A major confrontation between the Americans and the massed brigades of the North Vietnam Army would have been easy to handle; but the "nickel and dime" nighttime jungle skirmishes were almost impossible for the gigantic American military machine.

In those final days America was treated to pictures of surplus helicopters being dumped into the ocean, of a once impregnable embassy overrun with people trying vainly to get out, of the ill-equipped but victorious Viet Cong and their North Vietnamese counterparts occupying the city of Saigon. What had happened?

We simply didn't understand the nature of the battle or the enemy, some say. We didn't know the real cost of battling on the Asian mainland, and, worst of all, we didn't really know why we were there.

The passion with which our troops went was totally dissipated when they came home, and the result was bitterness and years of regret. Where have we seen that futile process before? In many other places, in many other times, with nations and individuals.

Such was the case of Samson, for example, who enjoyed a series of spectacular victories in his day. Brute strength—a gift from God—had carried him from one success to another. He effectively intimidated the enemies of Israel, and as long as Samson was able to perform, the people of Israel slept well at night.

But on another day there was another kind of battle. Unlike the rugged confrontations when Samson had faced large numbers of well-equipped soldiers and had destroyed them with ease, there was Delilah, a new enemy of sorts. Who would have thought that within her embrace lay the seeds of Samson's defeat?

The public life of Samson seemed to be marked with invincibility. But his private life was slowly being eaten away by a relationship that—while obviously special and enjoyable to him—was destructive to his passion to be a servant of God.

Samson certainly was warned; he was given more than one opportunity to face up to his increasingly vulnerable situation. But because Delilah gained an important position in his inner life, he chose to ignore the signals, and he was destroyed. Delilah's house became Samson's Vietnam experience.

The person who sets out to serve God must understand that a kind of guerrilla warfare is going on all around us. All too often the spiritual passion needed to carry on the strong life of a leader is dissipated by surrounding battles, battles we have never taken time to adequately understand. The enemy of the spirit is so well camouflaged he is almost impossible to ferret out, much less destroy.

The maintenance, or the restoration, of our spiritual passion requires us to understand not only the *prevailing conditions* and the *people encounters* in which passion is sapped or destroyed but also the kinds of *spiritual battles* that will deny us the energy we need.

Let me isolate a few sample issues that regularly neutralize those who are in any kind of leadership. They are subtle issues, and they are difficult to identify and root out. They yield only to the exercises of spiritual discipline, to those occasions when we take time to locate the source from which we are taking fire. Frankly, I find some of the issues virtually nameless, and when I find names for them, I am embarrassed to admit even to myself that I can find them within me. *But they are there!*

In discussing these, I want to be clear that this is not even the start of an exhaustive list of all those issues that neutralize spiritual passion. They are actually issues with which I am more personally familiar. The value of listing a few and identifying them merely helps us all to think about the nature of our warfare and what it is doing to us.

FOUR SPIRITS THAT DESTROY SPIRITUAL PASSION

"The ministry would be a great calling if it weren't for people," we used to joke on a day when there had been a flow of people problems. For people are always the greatest struggle for someone in leadership—and, of course, the greatest point of joy.

We discussed together the effects of people upon us in a previous chapter. But what we need to look at now is the nature of relationships among those who are themselves leaders. Here is a special brand of spiritual warfare that often breaks out to our shame.

One of the great literary pieces that came out of the Vietnam War was a book called *Friendly Fire*. It detailed the events surrounding the death of a soldier and the failure of the defense department to account for what had actually happened. Only after the dead soldier's persistent parents

92

demanded disclosure did it become clear that the young man had not lost his life to the enemy but to misdirected artillery fire from American guns. Friendly fire, it was called.

Friendly fire is not unusual among Christian leaders. The wounds incurred in spiritual battle come, unfortunately, all too often from friendly guns. When we fire those guns at our fellow soldiers or receive fire from them, spiritual passion is often destroyed.

I have discovered that there are a number of ways this can happen. It is not an attractive list, and what makes it most painful for me is the realization that my finger has sometimes been on the trigger. Friendly fire comes in the form of several poisoned spirits. The first of those might be called the competitive spirit.

1. The Competitive Spirit

God has called us to work together. We are surrounded by people who are just as excited about their call to leadership as we are by our call. Who are these people? Either they can become our partners, our confidence builders, or they become our *competitors*. The former help build our spiritual passion; the latter, when we see them as competitors, drain it.

Right here we ponder together a most insidious form of spiritual warfare that has destroyed countless people. Diotrephes, "who likes to put himself first" (3 John 9 RSV), evidently saw the apostle John as a competitor and intercepted all the communications that John had sent to that congregation.

Think of it! The people were denied input from one of the beloved disciples of the Lord because one man reduced his relationship with John to the level of competition.

Being the American that I am, I grew up in a competitive environment. We men in particular were raised with the notion that everyone around us had to be measured to see who was the best. When we were kids, we compared our muscles, our running speeds, the quality of our baseball mitts, and the privileges our parents extended to us. When we were teenagers, we compared our cars, our social skills, our athletic prowess. And as men (now more and more the women have joined us) we are constantly tempted to match the size of our homes, the prestige and power of our jobs, and, strangely enough, the skills of our children (full circle).

Among Christian leaders the competition often continues. Pastors wrestle with feelings of ill will toward another whose congregation is larger; preachers and authors are tempted to compare another's public acceptance to their own; lay leaders suddenly find themselves looking to see who was, and who was not, invited to address or attend the myriad of seminars and conferences around the world today, and using these announcements as a sort of bellwether to determine who is in, and who is out, with the public.

When we get absorbed by a sense of competition, we are in danger. Our passion subsides as we spend more and more time jealously looking sideways at the roads others are taking rather than looking ahead at the path God has paved for us.

Henri Nouwen wrote of this sort of thing happening in another kind of world, that of the stage performer:

Recently an actor told me stories about his professional world which seemed symbolic of much of our contemporary situation. While rehearsing the most moving scenes of love, tenderness and intimate relationships, the actors were so jealous of each other and so full of apprehension about their chances to "make it," that the back stage scene was one of hatred, harshness and mutual suspicion. Those who kissed each other on the stage were tempted to hit each other behind it, and those who portrayed the most profound human emotions of love in the footlights displayed the most trivial and hostile rivalries as soon as the footlights had dimmed (Nouwen, *Reaching Out*, pp. 49–50).

"What about this man?" Peter asked Jesus of one of the other disciples. "What is that to you?" Jesus responded. "Follow me!" (John 21:21,22 RSV).

"Some preach the gospel (in the streets of Rome) out of a sense of competition against me," Paul wrote. But that's OK, he adds. At least the gospel is being preached (see Phil. 1:15–17).

The former is Jesus' way of telling Peter, don't think competitively; the latter is Paul's way of saying, I never worry about the success of others.

In Pearson's biography of Oscar Wilde, a discussion is recorded that centers on "the commonly-held view that the good fortune of one's friends makes one discontented."

Said Wilde: "The devil was once crossing the Libyan desert, and he came upon a spot where a number of small fiends were tormenting a holy hermit. The sainted man easily shook off their evil suggestions. The devil watched their failure, and then he stepped forward to give them a lesson. 'What you do is too crude,' he said. 'Permit me for one moment.' With that he whispered to the holy man, 'Your brother has just been made Bishop of Alexandria.' A scowl of malignant jealousy at once clouded the serene face of the hermit. 'That,' said the devil to his imps, 'is the sort of thing which I should recommend'" (Pearson, *Oscar Wilde*, pp. 127–28).

I discovered a brutal truth about myself, a rather frightening personal flaw, some years ago when I suddenly realized that I rarely delighted in another person's success. In my insecurity as a young pastor, I felt somehow that anyone else's success was a threat to my own. That's the competitive spirit showing.

Rather than delighting in the success and effectiveness of others, I automatically began to explain it away. "He has connections," I might say of one. "She received a lucky break she didn't deserve," it was possible to observe of another. "They liked his preaching only because he had a few well-placed jokes in the sermon." The list of possible rationalizations goes on. We pray for the church to grow, I found, and then we proceed to explain away the church that grows if it is not ours.

Rarely, I painfully discovered, did I ever say to myself, "that man (or woman) deserves praise for that article because it is indeed an excellent piece of writing, and it's a lot better than I could ever have done." Scarcely did it ever occur to me, in my natural state, to be thrilled over the fact that a brother or a sister in faith had achieved something marvelous for the community of believers. How could I say in my heart that I was committed to the expansion of Christ's kingdom since I failed to rejoice when I heard of others in concert with God's Spirit making it happen?

How did I make this discovery about myself? I suspect it came about because I noted how few peers found it possible to express delight in any sort of success I might be enjoying.

96

It was easy to see the competitive spirit in them; it wa[ ]dreadful, and I mean utterly humiliating, when I discovered that I was the same sort of person. A painful realization! And my competitive feelings had to be rooted out before I could enjoy the spiritual passion God wanted me to have.

Ralph Turnbull recalled an incident recorded in one of my favorite biographies, *Henry Varley's Life Story*. Varley was a great preacher in England's latter nineteenth century. A neighboring pastor had begun to draw some members of Varley's congregation to his services because of his gift as an expositor of the Scriptures. Henry Varley discovered that deep within him he nurtured a serious resentment toward the other man.

> I shall never forget the sense of guilt and sin that possessed me over that business. I was miserable. Was I practically saying to the Lord Jesus, "Unless the prosperity of thy church and people comes in this neighborhood by me, success had better not come"? Was I really showing inability to rejoice in another worker's service? I felt that it was sin of a very hateful character. I never asked the Lord to take away my life either before or since; but I did then, unless his grace gave me victory over this foul image of jealousy (Turnbull, *A Minister's Obstacles*, p. 39).

2. The Critical Spirit

The competitive spirit was not the only poisoned spirit I found in the recesses of my inner life. A critical spirit that often squelches spiritual passion also lurked inside. It was there, in abundance, and while I despised it in others, I was embarrassed to discover it was also ready and waiting in me. When tired or unguarded, I found it easy to find a flaw in every person in my world. I found something to carp about in the reading of every magazine or in the watching of or listening to a Christian presentation on television or radio.

The tendency to emphasize the negative in every situation, to find the ideological or doctrinal difference, to see the character fault, to major in locating the weakness of the program prevented me from generating the positive energy I needed to get on with my part of the work to which I'd been called.

I have a vivid memory of visiting a major city in another country where I was the guest of missionaries. During the days I was there, I was impressed with two things: first, the relative ineffectiveness of their common work, and, second, the critical appraisal fellow missionaries had for one another. It seemed as if every conversation I had with anyone was marked with criticism of another's philosophy or strategy. So poisoned did the atmosphere seem that I found myself counting the hours until the wheels of my plane would lift off the ground to take me away.

Perhaps it was my problem, but in attempting to minister to them from the Scriptures, as I had come to do, I felt stifled and impotent to offer them anything helpful. It was as if each was separated from the others by invisible walls. Together they sang and prayed; apart they criticized and diminished one another.

The good men and women of that area of the world had all gone there at great personal sacrifice to engage in the expansion of Christ's kingdom through evangelism and church planting. How excited and motivated they must have felt when they first arrived, like the Americans who first hit the beaches in Vietnam.

But now an insipidness characterized their combined energy level. It was friendly fire all over again: more attention riveted upon fellow soldiers than upon the frontline where spiritual warfare was actually taking place. Looking back I realize that what I was experiencing was the *absence* of spiritual passion, in them and then in me, an energy nullified by critical spirit.

3. The Vain Spirit

A third poisoned spirit that destroys spiritual passion makes its presence known when we harbor an insatiable need to impress people in order to have them prefer or like us. This is an inner need that usually arises from private insecurities. We are driven to weigh every word and action in terms of how it will affect people's feelings about us. The passion to impress others overcomes the passion to advance the interest of Christ.

No leader can skip over this one lightly. It is my observation that most would-be leaders have deep insecurities that make them very sensitive to what the crowd thinks about them.

The need to impress emerges in a score of ways: by the way we insist that proper credit be given to our accomplishments, by the attention we pay to titles and privileges, and by the amount of attention we bring to ourselves in conversations.

"Listen to yourself," my wife, Gail, tells me often as we enter a group of people. "Don't fall into the trap of thinking that you have to tell people everything you know. Let them be heard about things in their world. You've enjoyed enough attention for one day. Besides, I'm impressed with you; that's all you need!"

The more we seek to impress others about ourselves, the more security we will develop built around human adulation. And the less God will feel obligated to provide us with

His gift of security. The more we strive to live off the applause of others, the less we will hunger for the passion that causes us to seek the approval of the heavenly Father.

The great theologian James Denny once wrote, "No man can bear witness to Christ and to himself at the same time. No man can give the impression that he is clever and that Christ is mighty to save."

4. The Adversarial Spirit

Our spiritual passion will also be affected by how we handle adversarial relationships. I'm thinking of our critics: those who are friendly and those who are unfriendly. And I'm thinking of those who have opposed or failed us and toward whom we feel vengeful.

The adversarial spirit is a poisoned spirit, and it creates an energy of bitterness that will destroy every ounce of spiritual passion we have.

A. B. Bruce wrote of Alcibiades who had been a disciple of Socrates but then became his enemy. Alcibiades recorded his own feelings of resentment and yet reluctant admiration:

> I experience toward this man alone [Socrates] what no one would believe me capable of, a sense of shame. For I am conscious of an inability to contradict him, and decline to do what he bids me; and when I go away I feel myself overcome by the desire of popular esteem. Therefore I flee from him and avoid him. But when I see him, I am ashamed of my admissions, and often times I would be glad if he ceased to exist among the living; and yet I know well that were that to happen, I should be still more grieved (Bruce, *The Training of the Twelve*, p. 371).

I think I know just a little bit about the meaning of hate. I would have denied it at the time, but looking back, I now know that I sometimes have been guilty for short periods of serious feelings of vengeance toward a person or two who, I felt, wronged me. At least that was my perception. On those occasions I was so overcome with adversarial feelings that I did not stop to think how I may have been wrong. That's a serious error.

One memory that burns deep within is that of a plane flight on which I was headed toward a meeting that would determine a major decision in my ministry. I knew I was in desperate need of a spiritual passion that would provide wisdom and submission to God's purposes. But the passion was missing because I was steeped in resentment toward a colleague.

For days I had tried everything to rid myself of vindictive thoughts toward that person. But, try as I might, I would even wake in the night, thinking of ways to subtly get back at him. I wanted to embarrass him for what he had done, to damage his credibility before his peers. My resentment was beginning to dominate me, and on that plane trip I came to a realization of how bad things really were. I could hardly pray; I could hardly think clearly about the future.

As the plane entered the landing pattern, I found myself crying silently to God for power both to forgive and to experience liberation from my poisoned spirit. Suddenly it was as if an invisible knife cut a hole in my chest, and I literally felt a thick substance oozing from within. Moments later I felt as if I'd been flushed out. I'd lost negative spiritual weight, the kind I needed to lose; I was free. I fairly bounced off that plane and soon entered a meeting that did in fact change the entire direction of my life. I have often wondered what would have happened to me if I'd gone to

101

that meeting with the excess weight of hate still in my heart. Would I not have been nailed, fixed to that point in my personal history and not permitted to move ahead under the leadership of the Spirit of Christ?

Spiritual passion cannot coexist with resentments. We can do our best to claim that we are in the right, but the Scriptures are clear. The unforgiving spirit is no home to the energy that causes Christian growth and effectiveness.

Learning to accept the harsh or gentle criticism of others who may or may not like us is a heavy discipline also. "There is a kernel of truth in every critique," I was taught by a mentor; "Look for it, and you'll be a better man."

Usually, in the past, I wasn't looking; I tended to be too busy ducking in self-defense. But as the time came when I could actually cultivate appreciation for criticism, my spiritual passion was enhanced.

Now I am impressed by the fact that virtually everything of value I have learned has come from the mouths of my critics: both those who care for me and those who feel animosity toward me. When we look for the kernel of truth, we find growth, effectiveness, and room for spiritual passion.

Friendly fire is a serious matter, whether given or received. It usually maims good people and leaves them unfit for the real battles of life. Is there anything sadder than a passionate soldier who went off to battle but returned dispirited—wounded by his own people? The passion he took to the battlefield is missing when he returns. We need to brood over that picture with serious intention. It suggests why many of us are living joylessly in our work for God.

9

He Knew I Couldn't Handle It!

An inky and mysterious spiritual world lies within us. An inner space that may be as expansive and unexplored as outer space. And in that strange and awesome abyss there dwell motives and values and responses that are almost impossible to define or predict.

The presence of God may dwell in this space if we are careful to offer it to His control. Neglecting that, however, we unwittingly offer that space to energies that are destructive and treasonous. The biblical writers called this *sin*, and they repeatedly warn of its power.

Weariness results from being constantly ambushed by that power. If we experience fatigue of the spirit from the conditions about us in the outer world, and if we are exhausted by the kinds of people with whom we have contact at certain times, then it is important to speak of this third origin of spiritual tiredness: the spiritual battles that find their inception deep within the human spirit.

Jesus warned:

For from within, out of the heart of man, come evil thoughts, fornication, theft, murder, adultery, coveting, wickedness, deceit, licentiousness, envy, slander, pride, foolishness. All these evil things come from within, and they defile a man (Mark 7:21–23 RSV).

Not a pretty description, but an accurate one. And if we do not take great care to shine a light regularly into that darkness to discover what lurks there, almost surely that spiritual attack will be relentless and debilitating.

Catherine Drinker Bowen has written an excellent biography of Sir Francis Bacon, the seventeenth-century Englishman who knew the heights and depths of honor and disgrace. A gifted man with an appetite for power and wealth, Bacon was driven from within to succeed and to gain prominence in the king's court. By hard work and wit he rose to the position of Lord Chancellor of England. Then at the peak of his career, he was impeached by Parliament for taking bribes while in office. Convicted, he was disbarred and banished from London. Bacon was a whipped, spiritually exhausted man.

Bowen recorded a prayer the deposed Lord Chancellor wrote in which he confessed the squandering of his life. From his words it becomes clear that Bacon realized he had ignored the one place in his world where there was power that could bring him down—the evil that ambushes from within. "So as I may truly say," he wrote, "my soul hath been a stranger in the course of my pilgrimage."

Bacon is telling us that a failure to light up the territory within is to invite a spiritual attack from the one place we can least afford to be vulnerable.

François Fénelon wrote of the importance of keeping light focused upon the inner world lest we become victimized like Bacon. But shining the light within may be a frightening experience, for when we do, there may be an unpleasant surprise.

As that light increased, we see ourselves to be worse than we thought. We are amazed at our former blindness as we see issuing forth from the depths of our heart a whole swarm of shameful feelings, like filthy reptiles crawling from a hidden cave. We never could have believed that we had harbored such things, and we stand aghast as we watch them gradually appear. But we must neither be amazed nor disheartened. We are not worse than we were; on the contrary, we are not better (Fénelon, *Spiritual Letters to Women*, pp. 21–22).

It is certainly not a flattering picture Fénelon paints of our inner worlds in his seventeenth-century description. But it is imagery that could be helpful when we begin to think of the "reptiles" within that fight the development of spiritual passion and seek to quench its force.

TWO INNER BATTLES THAT WAR AGAINST SPIRITUAL PASSION

We could not list the many battles initiated in the inner world. The best we can do is put the spotlight on a limited few of the issues a person in Christian leadership is likely to face. And we can establish greater vigilance over those things that, if left untouched, emerge at our most vulnerable times and nullify our attempts to develop a spiritual passion.

The Battle of Ambition

Take the incredible force of *ambition,* which shows its head at the strangest of times. Ambition is the urge to get ahead, to establish oneself powerfully and securely. It was the key to Lord Bacon's downfall.

105

Christian leaders are not expected to be ambitious. Somehow we have accepted a system in our community of believers that suggests it is usually proper for laypeople to pursue careers and vocations ambitiously, at least if they do not do it blatantly. There is nothing wrong, we imply, in a person's seeking or changing jobs for advancement and salary increases. As long as one keeps morally upright, relationally committed, and ethically clean, we are not disturbed by the reasonable concern to get ahead.

Now of course we would be shocked if a Christian pastor or missionary applied the same reasoning. No one would appreciate a pastor's telling his deacons or elders, "I am leaving this church because a larger, better-paying church has offered me a position." People in Christian service are simply not permitted to talk, or even think, that way. Or are they?

Ambition is a difficult spiritual enemy to pin down. It covers itself in devious ways. It can sneak in through vocabulary such as "the Lord has led me . . ." or "I have this vision for . . ." or "the door has been opened to. . . ."

Ambition can cloak itself in one's "burdens for . . ." or "concern toward. . . ." It can hide behind the effort to expel or unseat rivals because they hold divergent theologies.

But ambition is most dangerous when it settles into the cracks of the heart and tempts a person to weigh every situation in terms of the possibilities of advancing into positions where there is fame or reward.

A close parallel exists between raw personal ambition and the spiritually-passionate desire to advance the kingdom of Christ. Sometimes it is difficult at first to tell the difference between the two.

Simon the magician appeared in his early days of Chris-

106

tian conversion to be a humbled, repentent believer—until Peter and his colleagues came to town and displayed some remarkable gifts of the Spirit.

> Now when Simon saw that the Spirit was given through the laying on of the apostles' hands, he offered them money, saying, "Give me also this power, that any one on whom I lay my hands may receive the Holy Spirit" (Acts 8:18,19 RSV).

One should have known that the old showman who had dazzled people for years was still likely to have some of his original ambition for the crowd's affection. It had been there all the time just waiting to burst out. Apparently, he'd never shined the light within and found the enemy waiting for the right moment to attack. And when Peter came north to Samaria, the fight was on.

Peter was not particularly diplomatic in his handling of the exposed ambition of Simon: "Your heart is not right before God. Repent therefore of this wickedness of yours . . . that . . . the intent of your heart may be forgiven you" (Acts 8:21,22 RSV).

The intent of the heart is those hidden reptiles of which Fenelon spoke—in this case, the reptiles of ambition. You could say that since Simon had not shined the light into his own inner world, Peter did it for him.

Most of us who have entered Christian service as pastors *or* laypeople understand ambition. In our youngest years, ambition does its job upon us. We want to get ahead and seize opportunities in which we will be able to prove ourselves and our gifts.

Our service for Christ takes on twisted motives we find it difficult to sort out. We pray that the honor of God will be seen in our efforts, yet we are all too conscious that the approval of the crowd is at least of equal importance.

We claim that we do not wish to get ahead of God's purpose or His programs, yet we find within us a drive to take advantage of every situation to advance our own dreams and persuasions. We hear of openings, and we are tempted to manipulate ourselves into position to be considered. We crave the attention of notables and the invitations of organizations to participate in whatever capacity will provide a higher reputation.

My first congregation was a small group of lovable farmers in Western Kansas. To this day I hold all of them in the highest esteem for their faithfulness and loyalty to God and to one another. The congregation barely totaled forty on most Sunday mornings, and that was cut in half if we were in mud or harvest season. The church sanctuary and the parsonage across the road were seven miles north of the nearest paved road, almost twenty miles from the nearest town, not exactly Main Street, U.S.A.

We were genuinely happy serving that congregation during our seminary days. But my happiness did not disrupt my immature ambition, a hope that one day God would lift me up to "bigger things."

One hot July Sunday afternoon, I was walking across the section road to the church parsonage, pondering the possibility that God might one day do that lifting to bigger things.

Do I dare claim some sort of "section-road" revelation? For it was as if I heard God speak to me aloud in non-religious terms. Was it a voice within me or without? I don't know. But the message was plain. *Gordon, I will never permit you to play in the big leagues* (the bigger things) *until you have faithfully played in the little leagues.*

God had put the light deep within me and had exposed ambition, my discontent with where I was and what I was doing. It was a moment of confrontation, and I had to pause right there and confess what had been exposed. I made a promise before the day was over that I would live as if I were destined to remain serving that congregation for the rest of my life.

Some would say, perhaps, that I did indeed go on to bigger things as most pastors do. Strangely, today I do not feel as if I do anything that has any greater significance than what I did with those people in the country. In fact there are moments when Gail and I wonder what it would be like to return to the tranquillity of the farmland—ambition reversed!

Spiritual passion and ambition cannot share the same space. Young men and women painfully learn that. Older men and women who have never learned that suffer because they can never be satisfied with what they have.

Ambition is tiring; it overcomes spiritual passion and leaves one tired from the constant mental game playing that starts with "what-if" thoughts and goes on to "if-only" thoughts. A fatigue results from the dissatisfaction with where one is and what one is doing. We wonder why there isn't something better, and in the wondering we forfeit the desire to do well with *what is*.

The Holy Spirit's light shining within to expose ambition is a necessary thing.

The Battle of Pride

Akin to ambition is pride, the inability to handle success. Our Christian world includes men and women in both the pastoral and lay sectors who started into leadership not through the energy of ambition but by sincere commitment to God's purposes. But something happened along the way. Their success became intoxicating.

Uzziah, king of Israel, is a warning signal to us all. "As long as he sought the Lord," we are told, "God made him prosper" (2 Chron. 26:5 RSV). The man hit the top. He was successful in everything he did: the urban renewal of Jerusalem, the reorganization and reequipping of the army, and the invigoration of a sick economy. Nothing could go wrong except that which was deep within the darkness of the king's heart.

"When he was strong he grew proud, to his destruction," (2 Chron. 26:16 RSV) the reader is informed. And from there it was downhill. Uzziah died a leper in disgrace under the judgment of God.

Some years ago I had a conversation I've never forgotten. It was with a man I deeply admired for his skill in Bible teaching. Everyone who came into contact with him was impressed with his abilities. Yet throughout his adult life, he had never had the breakthrough into a larger ministry that some others have coveted. That perplexed me because I was convinced he had many superior gifts in comparison to others who were into the bigger things.

When I asked him whether he had ever resented the fact that greater opportunities had never come his way, his answer impressed me. "I know that God would not permit such things for me. He knows I would be unable to handle them." He was speaking of the temptation to pride. I admired the man for his frankness and for his self-awareness. And I came away, realizing how shackled a person can become if pride is not exposed and brought under control.

We watch the all too frequent crashes of leaders in our Christian community: men and women who are boosted by

110

the public to heights never thought possible before. The applause and the adulation are seductive and blinding. They generate pride in all but the most vigilant, and they effectively squelch spiritual passion, substituting for it the counterfeits of showmanship and charisma.

If we want to be men and women of spiritual passion, pride and ambition will have to be dealt with—harshly and repeatedly. They rarely surrender unconditionally. They hide in the interior jungles of inner space, emerging in the dark hours when no one suspects, when there is no light to expose their existence.

"He knew I couldn't handle it," my friend told me. I love the man for his honesty; I wonder what might have been.

10

It's What's Inside That Counts

A few years ago our country was shocked by a strange airplane accident. A well-known college football coach was flying in a private jet from the Midwest to the East Coast. There is some confusion as to the actual details, but during the flight, it became apparent to the ground controllers that the pilot was not flying according to a filed flight plan. Subsequent efforts to communicate with him failed.

Soon it was clear that both the pilot and his passenger were not conscious because of an oxygen deficiency or some other kind of malfunction. Eventually, the aircraft headed out over the ocean, the plane controlled only by autopilot. When the fuel was exhausted, the jet fell from the air.

Had you and I been standing on the ground looking upward as that small plane flew eastward, we would not have known that anything was wrong inside. Assuming that we could see it in its high flight, I might have been apt to say, "Look at that sleek jet. It sure is flying high and fast."

You might have said, "Can you imagine how important a person has to be in order to be flown around in a plane as expensive as that?"

Our impressions would likely have been quite positive until the plane began its exhausted descent to tragedy.

Then we might have reflected on how little we actually knew about what was going on inside.

Although the plane incident was unique in the annals of aviation history, a similar pattern in people's lives is not. In the Christian community there are men and women who, like the jet, appear to be flying high and fast. Every external sign suggests a straight and true course. Only when they run out of some sort of inner fuel and reveal their internal exhaustion do we realize that something was wrong.

Weary people. Action without passion. Words without substance. Perhaps we have touched one of the reasons so many people in our nation today claim faith but feel as if they make so little difference in their worlds.

The passionless life shows itself in the numbers of marriages and family relationships crumbling because the energy to overcome the things that separate and divide is no longer there. In the place of what was once fresh and dynamic is a staleness and boredom, a feeling of being trapped, the occasional desire to run.

Honest Christian men and women respond to the call to faith with a belief they have found what it means to integrate all the sectors of life in the lordship of Christ. But a few years later, they may be tempted to abandon their commitment because the resulting activity does not seem to fill a gaping emptiness still within. They are tired of words, of unfilled promises, of expectations never met.

I am constantly made aware of the relatively small knot of people in most churches and Christian groups who have paid a great price to serve, to hold things together for the benefit of the large numbers (the very nice people, we called them) who merely come and enjoy the fruits of it all. Those few are often tired; they grow restive, trying hard not to complain; and one by one they silently grapple with the

113

appealing prospect of calling it quits and letting someone else do the job. We have done them an injustice if we simply write them off as ones who couldn't finish the race.

I sat with a pastor who is my own age, and we spoke together of the dynamics of midlife. "I've been doing this for eighteen years," he says. "I have always believed that God wanted me to be a pastor. But there are times when I get tired of the words, sick of saying and doing the same old things over and over again while very little changes."

"Is it time to do something different?" I asked.

"I can't; I'm too set in my ways. And I don't have the slightest idea what I'd do. But what's worse, I don't know how much longer I can keep up the pace doing this."

Is there anything new or different about comments and problems of this sort? Many will say no. It is a matter of recommitment, some will say. A few will suggest the need for a good old-fashioned revival. I have good friends who will sincerely suggest a charismatic experience may be in order.

But I'm prepared to propose that there is indeed something new going on. I believe we are headed toward an epidemic of fatigue and weariness that never has been seen before. And in the first half of this book I've outlined some of the things that contribute to that contemporary exhaustion.

Christians have always worked hard. They have always known honest tiredness, the result of work and servanthood.

But something is different today. The believing community has never been so busy, never had so many voices to listen to, never so many choices to make, never so many ways to respond. That, I believe, explains why we are facing the potential of a wholesale exhaustion of the spirit. To ignore that unique phenomenon is to invite spiritual disaster.

I have spent half a lifetime listening to explanations of how to gain control and capability in spiritual things. On not a few occasions, I went away believing I had finally found the answer in the interpretations of one speaker or another. But my enthusiasm was usually dampened fairly quickly as I descended from the emotional high of the initial experience.

It only takes a few dashed expectations before one is tempted to give up trying. It is not that following the Lord isn't a desirable thing. This is no matter of doubting the basic biblical good news, the gospel of Jesus Christ. Nor is this a trip into theological deviation.

We are overwhelmed by the work of Christ on the cross. We are prepared to affirm that the power that raised Him from the dead is mightier than the power of all the stars combined. We delight to the stories of the early apostles and believers, and in the deepest levels of our hearts, we long for the same fervency and commitment—and of course for the powerful results!

But, for the most part and for most people, the fervency isn't there! And on the few occasions when it is, we fear it will too quickly disappear, and it often does.

Among the things that disappoint me the most is the sense that many Christians have hoped one too many times something would happen in their lives that would make them vibrant disciples of the Lord. But, with their hopes dashed, they have simply lost interest and made other things their chief target of interest. They are impervious to the promises of one more preacher, one more system, one more experience.

What we may have failed to see in the midst of all of this

contemporary religious and irreligious noise are a few simple facts consistent in the lives of holy men and women
down through the centuries.

Look inside their lives for secrets, and you will discover a
handful of things that defy system and definition. Just a few
principles that when followed seem to develop, maintain,
or renew spiritual passion.

11

Rack 'Em Up

The last time I remember having any serious amounts of extra time was during my university days. The simple lifestyle of a student meant that it was either work, study, or play. I opted frequently for play, and idle time was often spent with friends in the student union, the basement area where there were scores of pool tables. Leaning over each table were earnest young students, cue sticks in hand, searching for ways to knock one more ball into a corner or side pocket.

I headed for those tables many times to join friends for a game or two. Previous players would have left the table in a disheveled condition. Some balls would be in the pockets; others would be scattered across the table. It would be necessary to gather and realign all of them into a tight, triangular configuration at one end of the table.

To do that, one went to the wall on which hung a form, a simple wooden triangle called a rack. All of the balls were placed inside the form, those with a circle around them, alternating with those of a solid color. The black eight ball was placed in the center. Once the re-collected balls were in proper order, the form was lifted, and the players were ready to begin. "Your turn to break," someone would say,

117

pointing to a partner or an opponent. *Break* was a good description of what happened.

The designated breaker would approach the table and smack the white cue ball down the length of the table to crash against the balls, sending them in every direction. Instantly the balls were bashed apart! And the rest of the game involved picking them off one by one, sending each in its turn rolling toward a pocket.

Each time I brood upon that process which begins with a perfect triangular configuration of pool balls being systematically smashed apart, I see the typical cycle through which a busy person passes almost daily. In real life, the cycle begins with the forming of a dream and the amassing of spiritual passion. The cycle is further formed with a defined objective, a formal or informal plan of attack, and the matching of suitable capabilities and resources. And the action begins.

But as the hours pass, the fatigue and weariness I have previously described begins to set in. It is as if various environmental conditions, people (especially the VNP's and the VDP's), and spiritual realities, in and out of our control, come at us like cue balls, systematically threatening to bash the pieces of our lives apart. And if one is not paying attention, spiritual passion begins to drain away. We become aware that the dreams at the start, both large and small, are now foggy and illusive at best, dissipated at worst.

I don't mind admitting that this cycle from passion development to near passion dissipation has been a familiar picture in my own world. In the early days of my adult Christian commitment, the experience often demoralized me since no one had effectively communicated that this cycle was common to everyone. As one privileged to offer leadership in a family, in a church, and in various organizations, I know what it is like to reach a point where it is hard to care any longer about a dream or a vision. In such times it is as if the cue balls keep coming at me (internally *and* externally), and the bits of pieces of my life scatter like the balls on the pool table.

But at that same pool table we all might learn a valuable lesson for those busy moments when weariness begins to take its toll. The learning experience begins when the players reach for the rack to begin a new game. The scattered balls are collected again inside the rack, and the perfect triangular shape is re-formed.

That re-forming process is a picture of the experience that must happen regularly and systematically within those of us who want to maintain or, if necessary, restore our spiritual passion.

Why have we not fully understood that law of spiritual reality? We too are victims—by choice or by circumstance—of the cue balls in our personal history. Sometimes it is as if some monster took aim at us and cried Break!, and we feel hit from every side. Crushed, split, and propelled in directions we didn't wish to pursue, we frequently come to points where we are sure that we will never feel whole again.

After all of this discussion about weariness and passionlessness, is there anything positive to say? Are there principles and truths that, when properly applied, permit one to put the inner, and even the outer, life back into form in much the same way as we realign the pool balls at the beginning of a game?

I'm not asking about one more gimmick or simple formula like the kind we have been sold by enthusiasts. Nor am I asking for a method that appears to work for people of one temperament but not of another. Personally, my quest for answers moves in the direction of men and women of the past who seem to have found a simple basic secret relevant to all of God's people, regardless of generation or culture.

The early mystics called this exercise the act of *recollection*. Our English word *collect* is compounded with the prefix *re-* to suggest that there is a collection process that must happen over and over again because the breaks come so frequently.

Re-collection: those who have majored in the disciplines of the inner spirit have often seized upon that word as a description of what one does when there is a need for a renewal of spiritual passion. Hearing the word, I think of the act at the pool table. And I see it once again in the quiet but necessary actions of the heart: the recollection of the pieces of my being so that once again my inner self is a reservoir of spiritual passion, the energy that enables me to hear God's voice and to act as His child.

"I used to dislike the term 'to re-collect' as in 'to recollect oneself,' wrote Michael Quoist. "I thought it tired and deformed; it reminded me of angular, grey faces perched above scrawny necks more precarious than the tower of Pisa. But I rediscovered the term and find it quite marvelous now."

Quoist continued:

To recollect yourself is to recover all your scattered energies—those of the mind, the heart and the body. It is to reassemble all the pieces of yourself flung in the four corners of your past or the mists of your future, pieces clinging to the fringes of our desires (Quoist, *With Open Heart*, p. 245).

Most of us have neither time nor place for recollection in this busy life of ours—and thus the exhaustion. Recollec-

120

tion becomes a matter of priority *only* when we have experienced one too many times the tastelessness of a passionless life.

I recall an evening when the phone rang, and I was informed that there had been an auto accident and a man had been killed. Would I come quickly to the home to be with the spouse and children when the news was broken?

"I'm not ready for this," I remember thinking as I drove toward the home. "I'm empty; I have nothing to give." As I reviewed why I felt that way, it was clear that the reason lay in my failure for the past few days to have recollected myself so that when the times for true spiritual passion arose I would be prepared. How I got through the evening I will never know. Perhaps I drew on hidden resources, but I remember resolving that I would not be caught unprepared like that again.

Innumerable volumes have been written about inner realignment or recollection. Some have offered simple solutions; others have offered very complex and mysterious ones.

I would like to highlight three major themes in which I believe the recollective process happens. Each of the three demands a choice on our part: *to take time, to seek relationships, to set priorities.* And in the regularity of doing these things, spiritual passion overcomes weariness and provides the resolve one needs to pursue the kingdom lifestyle.

The three themes revolve around questions such as these:

QUESTION: *In what sort of places can recollection happen?* Are there any "consecratable" spaces in my life where I can form and enlarge my view of God, where I can discover the true size and eternal significance of things? ANSWER: in the

121

safe places where I am free from the disruptions and inter-ferences that corrupt the inner spirit.

QUESTION: *At what times might personal recollection hap-pen?* Are there moments in my personal schedule during which I must take a hard look at where I've been and where I am going? ANSWER: in the *still* or *sabbath times* of life.

QUESTION: *Who are the people or what are the relationships that both enforce my recollective experiences and benefit from them?* ANSWER: among those whom I call the *special friends* in my life.

QUESTION: *What happens as a result of the recollection experience?* What can one expect if the safe places, the still times, and the special friends form the core of daily experi-ence? ANSWER: the heart is retuned; heaven's signals are received; *spiritual passion is renewed.*

Break! shout the random, sometimes harsh, events of the day. Not until I have been formed and realigned, not until the parts of my life have been recollected and put into touch with the guiding hand and the whispering voice of the Spirit of God, will I cry, "Take your best shot. I may appear scattered for a moment, but I will always be in form."

12
Safe Places

My wife, Gail, and I were walking through the neighborhood one day, commenting on the appearance and architecture of various homes when I noticed a small but bright poster in one front window. It featured the silhouette of an open hand. The poster was obviously positioned in a prominent place where it could not be missed—even by a child. It was then that I learned that the simple emblem was indeed for a child.

"That poster is a sign of a safe place," Gail told me. It is a signal to a frightened or sick child that here is a home offering protection or assistance. If one only knocks on the door, there will be safety from trouble.

I immediately had a mental flashback to a time in my childhood when a safe place of that kind would have been a welcomed sight. I had accepted responsibility to deliver newspapers for a friend, and it took me into a strange neighborhood. The afternoon weather had suddenly turned cold, and I was poorly dressed to face the temperature change. I had no money to make a phone call to my home, and my parents had no idea where I was. But the papers had to be delivered.

Chilled to the bone, slowed down by the heavy weight of

123

the papers, and confused by poorly written directions and addresses, I remember coming to a point of total frustration. I needed assistance and had no idea where to get it. I felt absolute helplessness. It would have been a wonderful moment to have seen one of those posters with a hand on it. I needed a safe place, a warm place, a place to pull myself together and revive my flagging spirit.

We need safe places in our worlds. Not merely when we are in trouble but when we need to rest a bit, to regain our measure of spiritual passion and composure for the continuing challenges of the cue balls that constantly come at us.

No biblical character seems to have understood that better than King David of Israel. He was apparently acquainted with trouble and stress from the early years of his life. But he also appears to have coped well, perhaps because he understood the principle of the safe place.

As a young boy, David's father, Jesse, had given David responsibilities for tending the sheep. His objective was to care for and protect the family flock. That meant leading sheep to sites where quiet water, adequate pasture, and protective rest were available. It meant that David was to be guardian of the flock, standing between the sheep and their enemies when necessary. In short, as a shepherd, David was finder and guarantor of the safe places.

Later the boy became a soldier, and danger came not from wild animals or inadequate shelter, but from human enemies. And the matter of safe places took on new meaning.

Who knows what danger David was pondering when he wrote of the safe places and the protection of the shepherd from his childhood.

"The LORD is my shepherd," he wrote. ". . . he makes

me lie down in green pastures. He leads me beside still waters; he restores my soul" (Ps. 23:1,2 RSV). Here his perception of God was shaped by the view of a shepherd leading sheep into places of sustenance and safety. The result was the renewal of soul or spiritual passion, the lifting of weariness.

The image of a shepherd is a tender, most stimulating view of the Creator. It is a picture that our hustle-and-bustle view of life does not permit us to adequately contemplate or appreciate. Only those who come to understand the significance of safe places will fully appreciate what David is talking about.

Safe places were important to David when he felt vulnerable because of the consequences of his own sins and errors of judgment.

> I am surrounded by many troubles—
>   too many to count!
> My sins have caught up with me,
>   and I can no longer see;
> they are more than the hairs of my head,
>   and I have lost my courage.
> Save me, Lord! Help me now! (Ps. 40:12–13 TEV)

One pictures a man who could have used a window with a hand signaling a safe place.

David also lived with the relentless rivalry created by Saul. Later as king, David would be involved in many battles perpetrated by the annual invasions of Israel's enemies. Then serious family problems would crop up, many the result of his poor judgment as a father.

In all these situations, David knew what it was like to be on the run, seeking places of safety until he could gather strength and restore his fortunes. Read David's reflections about these times, and you will discover that he was looking first for *protection,* second, for strength or *renewal of soul,* and third, for the opportunity to *rebound.* Such excursions often took him to the desert where he could lose his enemies and find God.

A map of David's travels would probably reveal all sorts of localities that he would refer to as the safe places—mountain tops, caves, oases, and forest groves. To each of these places he would flee when under fire, and there he would stop for however long he needed to tend to his weariness.

In a larger sense, God's people have always adhered to a doctrine of safe places. The Garden of Eden was the ultimate safe place. In it there was no confusion, only order. Eden was a place where the glory and splendor of God were seen and appreciated. We are told that the first man and woman communed regularly with God in an intimacy that defies description. One imagines that there was an absence of weariness, both of body and spirit, as we have come to know it.

But Adam and Eve forfeited their right to that Edenic safe place, and before long they found themselves in a world marked with hostility and work of another kind. The labor they now gave to the earth produced only a fraction of the original abundance. Few places were now safe in any sense.

Succeeding generations had to deliberately create safe places in the form of altars, limited localities where for a short period they could reestablish their relationship with God. At the altar there was a moment of remembrance for special events or experiences. There was the sacrifice with the shedding of blood, reflecting the need for a reconciling action between God and the person. Supposedly one left the site of the altar newly invigorated and possessed of a sense of guidance for the future.

Abraham was a great safe-place builder, and a map of his travels would show altars all over the Promised Land where he encountered God, heard the voice of reassurance, and was provided direction and wisdom for the next set of challenges.

When Moses had lived eighty years, God called him to a safe place in the desert known by us as the burning bush. "Take off your shoes," God said, "for you are standing on holy ground" (Exod. 3:5 TLB). And from that safe place came a word from God that sent Moses off to confront the Pharaoh of Egypt. Later Moses would ascend Mount Sinai, another safe place, and engage in a series of conversations out of which would come the law and other instructions about a new way of life.

Soon the Hebrews had another kind of safe place, the tabernacle, built according to carefully given instructions. The specifications of this safe place reflected all sorts of truths about God and His promises. You apparently couldn't go near it without being reminded of something pertaining to God's covenant with His people. This tabernacle was always located in the center of the community. Everyone knew that it was the place to go when you had personal, spiritual turbulence or a need for reconciliation with God. A priest would be there to receive you or your family. You could always see the hand on the poster in the window.

Before the people crossed into the Promised Land, they came upon another safe place, Gilgal. Three things seemed to have transpired at Gilgal. First, an altar of stones was erected to commemorate what God had done in the mirac-

127

ulous crossing of the Jordan. Joshua then told them the altar would always be a place of remembrance, a reminder of how God brought us over into a new land.

Gilgal was, second, a place of reaffirmation of the special relationship God had with the Hebrews. The men of the nation were circumcised, a physical sign since the days of Abraham of their positive response to God's call. And third, while in Gilgal Joshua and his people received instructions as to how they were to defeat the city of Jericho in battle. The instructions were a strange, but nevertheless effective, battle plan. Gilgal is a classic safe place—a place of rest, remembrance, reaffirmation, and redirection.

The temple became a safe place many generations later. It was to have been a place of prayer for the nations, Jesus would later say. That was why he was so upset when he saw a safe place changed into a "den of thieves": a noisy and exploitive place, a congested shortcut people could take from one side of the city to the other (see Matt. 21:13). Additionally, the temple had become a marketplace where tired travelers were often swindled in their attempt to exchange foreign money for special offerings and the purchase of animals for sacrifice. A safe place had become the most dangerous of places.

Today the closest thing to a safe place that would pop up into our minds would be the church building where we regularly go to worship. And so it can be.

Henri Nouwen wrote in this vein when he said:

When you look out over the city of Rome, walk in its streets, or ride in its buses, you quickly realize that it is a crowded city full of houses, full of people, full of cars, yes—even full of cats. You see men and women moving quickly in all directions, you hear joyful and angry voices mixed with a great variety of street sounds, you smell many odors—especially cappuccino—and you feel the Italian embrace by which you gain a friend or lose your money. It is a busy, congested city, in which life manifests itself in all its boisterous intensity.

But in the midst of this lively and colorful conglomeration of houses, people and cars, there are the domes of Rome pointing to the places set apart for the Holy One. The churches of Rome are like beautiful frames around empty spaces witnessing to him who is the quiet, still center of all human life. The churches are not useful, not practical, not requiring immediate action or quick response. They are tranquil spaces, strangely empty most of the time. They speak a language different from the world around them. They do not want to be museums. They want to invite us to be silent, to sit or kneel, to listen attentively, and to rest with our whole being.

A city without carefully protected empty spaces where one can sense the silence from which all words grow, and rest in the stillness from which all actions flow, such a city is in danger of losing its real character (Nouwen, *Clowning in Rome*, pp. 37–38).

Spiritual passion can be renewed in such places. These domes of silence, as Nouwen calls them, can be our homes as if they had a hand in the window inviting us to protection, rest, and redirection. But, sadly, they often are not those sorts of places. They could be and should, but often they are not.

What Henri Nouwen describes as a place of silence and stillness "from which all things grow" is exactly what I mean when I talk about a safe place. But when the cathedral or the church fails us, other safe places can be just as useful and effective.

129

The consummate safe place is the heavenly one. The evangelist John was permitted to peek through the door in a vision, we are told in Revelation 4 and 5. Working hard to record his impressions, he wrote of the heavenly family about the throne of God.

First, there was activity regarding the being of God: "Holy, Holy, Holy," they sang in praise to the Mighty One (Rev. 4:8 RSV). Then, there was reflection on the great acts of God: "Thou didst create all things" (Rev. 4:11 RSV).

From there the family of God moved to ponder the aton-ing work of God in Christ: "Who is worthy to open the scrolls?" (Rev. 5:2 RSV) is the towering question. Then "I saw a Lamb" (Rev. 5:6 RSV) John wrote, and he wept as he saw the mystery of it all. Finally, the people of heaven are seen in their exaltation of the triumphant work of God, for they had "made them a kingdom of priests" (Rev. 5:10 TEV). It is a remarkable display of safe-place action. Perhaps it is meant to be an ideal picture for the reader of what sorts of things ought to happen when we enter safe places in our world.

The ancient Christian mystics (and a few modern ones) thought that safe places of any value could only be erected in obscure localities. So they built monasteries and her-mitages out in deserts, on mountain tops, or in forests. Hoping to find that spot where God could be touched and worshiped, they sometimes abandoned civilization: the noisy city streets, the cries of enraged people, and the clanging sounds of men and women at work or play.

But, as Michael Quoist points out, that may not have been a necessary venture (if even possible) for them or us:

I've always dreamed of solitude, the hermit's life, a cabin in the woods or a tiny chalet on the edge of a mountain.

I've always dreamed of deserts and silence. But I've resisted the dream, with the exception of one time when I offered myself the luxury of a retreat with a hermit: four hours by foot, far from any living creature and a hermit happy to see me. We talked a lot.

I understood then that I carry my hermitage around with me and that I don't need to go too far to meet my Lord. I often need to withdraw into my retreat, *if only for a few minutes. Christ waits for me there* (Quoist, *With Open Heart*, p. 155).

Frank Laubach came to understand the need for safe places in his world.* In his journal he reflected:

Are you building sacred palaces for yourself? I meant to write "places" to be sure, but I think I shall leave the word "palaces" for that is what any house becomes when it is sacred. The most important discovery of my whole life is that one can take a little rough cabin and transform it into a palace just by flooding it with thoughts of God. When one has spent many months in a little house like this in daily thoughts about God, the very entering of the house, the very sight of it as one approaches, starts associations which set the heart tingling and the mind flowing. I have come to the point where I must have my house, in order to write the best letters or think the richest thoughts.

So in this sense one man after the other builds his own heaven or his hell. It does not matter where one is, one can at once begin to build heaven, by thoughts which one thinks while in that place . . . I have learned the secret of heaven building—anywhere (Laubach, *Frank Laubach*, p. 27).

---

*Some of us may have a problem with the precision of Dr. Laubach's theology, but remember that he is speaking in mystical terminology as he seeks to express his sense of a safe place.

What have these men learned? Safe places can be any-where. "I don't need to go far," Quoist wrote. And Laubach turned a cabin into a "palace" by filling it with thoughts of God.

Can we transform hostile places into momentary safe places merely by declaring them so? Can a bus seat become a safe place? an automobile stopped in a rush-hour traffic jam? an office between appointments? a sickroom where a mother waits over a suffering child? a sidewalk during a stroll? a lunch counter before a class? Are we not learning that men and women can build altars any place—if not altars in the street, then altars in the heart; if not for an entire day, then for ninety seconds.

People who create safe places with regularity do not have to worry about weariness. Or when it comes, a visit to the safe place dispels it. Those who are constantly weary are those who think they can always move forward with no pauses, that they can always endlessly achieve with no rests at the safe places.

Some time ago Gail and I were driving along a busy freeway. In the car with us was a special friend, a man known to people around the world. He shared the fact that he was very tired and not a little frightened about an up-coming assignment later that day. Additionally, he admit-ted to great feelings of loneliness because his wife was ill and unable to be with him.

It was rush hour; the car was moving in the start-and-stop rhythm of heavy traffic. From the backseat Gail sud-denly said, "Gordon, let's intercede for————right now." The car immediately became a safe place. Jesus was there; we invited His presence. First Gail prayed, and then I— with my eyes open, of course.

Later our friend shared with others the meaning of that

moment and its restorative value to him. Rush hour, a car, a busy schedule—but we'd created an instant safe place. We had put a hand in the window.

When we drive across the country, we frequently check the map for upcoming rest stops. Here and there along the line of our route on the map are tiny rectangles. The map key says that these rectangles represent places for fuel, food, and rest. The travelers count the miles until they reach the turnoff marked REST STOP. It is the safe place for road-weary travelers.

The biographical maps of holy men and women are marked with countless rectangles: the places they made safe by meeting Christ there. Or should I say, the places Christ made safe by meeting them there. On such occasions they saw the hand in the window. Their safe places did not need to be beautiful cathedrals; they could be in the public square or even in the waiting area of the coliseum where they awaited a coming encounter with the lions. The roar of the crowd meant danger. But the Spirit of God meant, strangely enough, safety.

13

The Place of Secrets

Sir William Osler is among the most highly esteemed physicians in modern medical history. The classic two-volume biography of Osler abounds with stories depicting not only his genius as a practitioner of medicine but also his unusually compassionate nature.

It is said that one day he entered the pediatric ward of a London hospital and noted with delight the children who were playing at one end of the room. Then his gaze was drawn to one small girl who sat off to one side alone on her bed, a doll in her arms. She was clearly oppressed by feelings of loneliness.

A question about her to the head nurse brought the response that she was ostracized by the other children. Her mother was dead, Osler was told; her father had paid but one visit, bringing at that time the doll, which she now tightly clutched. Apart from that one visit, no one had ever come to see her again. As a result, the other children, concluding that she was unimportant, had treated her with disdain.

Sir William was at his best in moments like that, and he immediately walked to the child's bed. "May I sit down, please?" he asked in a voice loud enough to carry to where the other children were at play. "I can't stay long on this visit, but I have wanted to see you so badly." Those describing the moment say that the girl's eyes became electric with joy.

For several minutes the physician conversed with her, now in quiet, almost secretive tones. He inquired about her doll's health and appeared to be carefully listening to its heart with his stethoscope. And then as he rose to leave, his voice lifted again so that everyone heard, "You won't forget our secret, will you? And mind you, don't tell anyone." As Osler left the room, he turned to see the once-ignored youngster now the center of attention of every other child on the ward.

I would like to think that the wise physician created a safe place with the child for a moment, shared a secret or two, and restored her personal passion for life. His attentiveness and intimacy affirmed her specialness in her own eyes and the eyes of others.

The tender encounter between Osler and the child provides for me a parable about a life in intimate touch with God. We are all children at one point or another in our experience. Perhaps we are always children and don't wish to admit it. Sometimes we feel alone; at other times we are weary from our futile attempts to succeed or improve our lot; on yet other occasions our sense is that of complete vulnerability before the critic or the rival. We come to crave the safe place, a refuge where we can restore our strength, gain our bearings, and begin again.

"There is a place of quiet rest," the poet Cleland McAfee wrote, "near to the heart of God. A place where sin cannot molest." It can be a place to meet the One whom Helmut Thielike called *The Waiting Father*. No one can live well without such places; but many try.

Psalm 63 is a poem about safe places. Some believe that the early church sang the words of this psalm at almost every worship service as they gathered in the safe place of congregational meeting, away from the stress of the world.

The psalm was written with the desert in mind, and it is likely that it was written while the writer was in the desert, fleeing from a dangerous enemy. Some believe the author, David, was running from Saul, the increasingly deranged king who saw the young shepherd boy as a rival to his throne. Others, including myself, believe that the psalm was constructed when David was in flight from Jerusalem after his son staged a sudden coup.

If Psalm 63 was written in the second of these two possible contexts, then I come to an even better appreciation of the words "And the king . . . arrived weary at the Jordan; and there he refreshed himself" (2 Sam. 16:14 RSV). The psalm would give a strong indication of just how David went about refreshing himself.

And how did he do it? He declared the wilderness where he found himself to be a safe place. There the young man on the run entered into a time of personal intimacy with the waiting Father.

"O God, thou art my God, I seek thee, my soul thirsts for thee; my flesh faints for thee, as in a dry and weary land where no water is" (Ps. 63:1 RSV). The writer had looked about and matched the state of his inner being with the environment. My private world is much like the desert; there is thirst and terrible weakness of spirit, the absence of spiritual passion.

Apparently stripped of everything, David turned to the state of his inner being. He could afford to lose the resources of his outer or public world, but he was smart

136

enough to know that he could not go much further if his private world was empty.

Wherever the writer was, he had stopped everything: running, fighting, panicking. He had entered a safe place and called for the Lord's presence. His desert could have been a modern office, a living room, a picnic table. All that counted was that he had announced his intention to meet with his God.

It is fascinating what David did with special imagery. He set his imagination running freely, seizing past experiences in which he had communed with God and renewed his spiritual passion.

FOUR KINDS OF SAFE PLACES THAT RENEW SPIRITUAL PASSION

At least four different experiences came to his mind as he sought to regain the energy of the spirit. And each provides an insight both to what a safe place can actually be and to what sorts of themes one is liable to hear when God whispers secrets in the safe places.

1. The Sanctuary

There are no buildings in a wilderness, certainly no temples or churches. And yet it seems clear that David had a craving to enjoy an experience in the sanctuary. All his life he had understood the meaning of sanctuaries: first, as a shepherd when he created fortified places for his sheep, then as a soldier when he learned to seek strongholds or high places. As king in Jerusalem, the sanctuary at the

137

tabernacle became a place for spiritual retreat, a place where he joined the congregation to worship.

But the sanctuary in Jerusalem was far away; it was only a memory. But David had gone there so many times in the past that it became possible to create an imaginary sanctuary in his private world. There in the desert he could walk right into a specially designed sanctuary that offered the possibility of personal renewal. "So I have looked upon thee in the sanctuary, beholding thy power and glory. Because thy steadfast love is better than life, my lips will praise thee" (Ps. 63:2–3 RSV).

The significance of these words grows when one remembers that the writer was greatly threatened. Whether you believe that he was on the run from Saul or Absalom, the issue is the same. David had been overwhelmed by a human power greater than he was. How should he cope with this? How did every great man or woman of God in the Bible cope with the issue of momentary defeat or threat? They set their inner beings on the power and glory of God, a power much greater than anything in the world. And when the contrast is made, all things become reduced to true size.

David entered the imagined sanctuary just as he had done in the real one so many times in the past. And the first message that came to him was God's majesty and glory. When he finished this experience of worship, his fear was abated; he was in touch with reality once again.

This experience was Daniel's when he was under the death threats of King Nebuchadnezzar. His prayer revealed his preoccupation: "He changes times and seasons; he removes kings and sets up Kings" (Dan. 2:21 RSV). It was a prayer of reorientation that focuses on true power and true majesty.

The same thing happened with the early church when

Peter and John returned fresh from the cease-and-desist threats of the Jerusalem city leadership. What was their prayer in the sanctuary? "Sovereign Lord who didst make the heaven and the earth. . . . look upon their threats" (Acts 4:24,29 RSV).

The weariness that comes from intimidation or defeat, the fatigue that comes from being drained by people who attempt to dominate our world, and the exhaustion that comes from fighting spiritual battles need to be cast in the context of the God of ultimate might and strength. And that is exactly what David did in his safe place. It became a sanctuary for eternal perspectives.

In this sanctuary David not only perceived the greatness of the majesty and power of God, but he was also refreshed with the reassurance of the steadfast love of the Lord: "Because thy steadfast love is better than life, my lips will praise thee" (Ps. 63:3 RSV).

If this psalm came out of the tragedy with Absalom, then David had a right to brood in the desert about the meaning of loyalty, not only from his family but also from his countrymen who had turned him out of power. At one time they had cheered him on in battle; they had applauded his efforts as king. But now many of them had abandoned him for the silver-tongued Absalom who had out-promised David.

What did David have now? Only the reminder, in this sanctuary of the desert, that God's love for him was steadfast. To put it in the words of a later prophet, Jeremiah: "The steadfast love of the LORD never ceases, his mercies never come to an end; they are new every morning; great is thy faithfulness" (Lam. 3:22,23 RSV).

No person in any form of leadership is going to go on forever without certain feelings of betrayal or terrible loneliness. And if leaders put their trust in the applause or loyalty of human beings, a terrible letdown will likely result.

For such people a safe place like David's sanctuary becomes emphatically important. Here things are regularly brought to true size, and here there is a reminder of the loyal love of God. It is God's secret between Himself and the one seeking sanctuary. And it is heard only in the safe place. And having heard the secret over and over again in the safe place, one has never to panic over the loyalty or disloyalty of people who can often make serious errors of judgment and strip the leader of everything. David knew.

2. The Night Room

As David pondered his outer world in the desert, a second kind of safe place came to mind. There too he had met God in the past. It was his place of rest, where he usually slept, the night room in his palace. "As I lie in bed, I remember you; all night long I think of you, because you have always been my help" (Ps. 63:6,7 TEV).

Although his private quarters were geographically back in Jerusalem, David reconstructed them in the desert where he felt the need for surroundings speaking of safety.

Now the theme in the night room, this second kind of safe place, is *the helpfulness of God,* a theme that had been at the root of David's spiritual thinking all his life. When the helpfulness of God was real to him, his spiritual passion was renewed and unlimited. Most of us would have preferred to use such moments to strengthen our bitterness, to erect defenses, and to recruit and motivate the people who would help get back what has been lost. Not David. It was a time for safe-place reflection.

David reflected upon the helpfulness of God on the day

when he had stood before Saul, discussing the giant Goliath. He had volunteered to take on Goliath, and Saul was
ready for any sort of proposed solution, no matter how zany
it seemed.

How could David dare to think that he could handle
Goliath? The young man spoke of his shepherding days,
the moments when the flock was attacked by lions and
bears. On every occasion David had handled such enemies.

How had he done it? "The LORD who delivered me from
the paw of the lion and from the paw of the bear, will
deliver me from the hand of this Philistine." He must have
been believable because Saul said, "Go, and the LORD be
with you" (1 Sam 17:37 RSV).

And the Lord had been with David. History has told the
story over and over again: one dead giant. The Lord was
with David.

Over and over again in the quietness of the nighttime
hours, David had lain upon his bed thinking of times like
those. Over and over again in that safe place, he had heard
the words of God: *I will be your help*. And now out on the
desert he was prepared to create a safe place like his night
room in Jerusalem where he could once again hear the same
promise.

When our daughter, Kristy, was five years old, the room
where she slept was a safe place to her, but only if it was
carefully arranged before she fell into sleep. I remember her
earnest instructions before I would leave her. Her dolls and
stuffed animals had to be lined up against the wall in a
carefully prescribed order, each one having its nightly turn
to be tucked in with her. The window shade had to be
lowered to a set point: no lower, no higher. The top sheet
had to be folded over the edge of the blanket. And, finally,
the bedroom door had to be left open just far enough so that

141

it admitted the glow of the night light in the hall but not so that the direct light would shine into her eyes as she slept.

The final words as I said goodnight were always, "Daddy, where will you be, and what time are you going to bed?" And after I answered her questions, she would remind me, "Now don't you go to sleep before I'm asleep."

In her childhood, the bedroom would be a safe place if all the routines were properly established. Then she could drift off to sleep comfortably confident that everything was under control and that her mother and dad were nearby to provide protection if it were needed.

I hear David relating to the same thing. He seems to be saying: *In the night hours when I am at rest, I am reminded that "you have always been my help." I know where you are, and I know that you're not asleep.*

In the tidal wave of a day's events and experiences, many of us even though we are busy and preoccupied, stop and create a safe place like David's sleeping room. And for a moment we ponder the reminder that God will be our help. We may even ask of Him, "Where will you be?" and we are apt to hear His whisper that settles the troubled heart and renews lost passion: "I will be with you; I will not fail you or forsake you" (Josh. 1:5 RSV).

3. The Protective Wings

Not too many living things can be easily seen at first glance in a desert. Only with a studied look will one spot insects, reptiles, rodents, and small, fast-moving animals. But one will always see the birds—hovering, spiraling about on the air currents, darting occasionally to the ground to pick off quarry. They are free to sing.

Birds understand safe places; that's how they survive.

142

Safe places in the air *above* the danger, in well-placed nests *away* from the danger, and close to protective parents' wings *covered* or *lifted* from the danger.

As David brooded upon safe places, the wings of a bird came to mind.

Those in trouble seek safe places where they can get back their courage, their hope, their desire to return to the battle. In the safe place they will think about the higher power that is greater than the power that now threatens them. They will consider the meaning of love and loyalty that does not wane or turn on them. And they will think about where help might come from.

But sooner or later they are apt to think about protection. And that's where the birds come in. Birds raise the issue of protection, and in protected places one feels free to rejoice, to laugh, to sing.

When was the last time, David might have wondered, when he was free to sing? Perhaps as he asked these questions, David began to recall the many times he had seen parent birds with outstretched wings offering protection to their young. And he was caused to write: "In the shadow of thy wings, I sing for joy" (Ps. 63:7 RSV).

The wings of the parent bird are a theme in Scripture, a theme always speaking of protection and care. Moses, like David, had watched birds in action and used them to remind his people of God's protective concern for them as he made them into his people: "Like an eagle teaching its young to fly, catching them safely on its spreading wings, the LORD kept Israel from falling" (Deut. 32:11 TEV).

Moses had obviously watched the parent eagle push the eaglets out of the nest to force them into flying lessons. But had the tiny eaglet failed to use its wings properly and begin flight, its parent would have swooped under the falling youngster and caught it on outstretched wings. The upper surface of the wing meant protection when falling.

A psalmist seized the theme of the wings of a bird and wrote: "He will cover you with his wings; you will be safe in his care; his faithfulness will protect and defend you" (Ps. 91:4 TEV).

The underside of the parent bird's wings provided protection from enemies on the ground or near the nest. Jesus Himself alluded to the birds when He talked passionately to the people of Jerusalem on the purpose of His redemptive love: "How many times I wanted to put my arms around all your people, just as a hen gathers her chicks under her wings, but you would not let me!" (Matt. 23:37 TEV). The wings spoken of by our Lord appear to speak of warmth, nurture, and rest—protective elements.

David himself had thought of bird's wings on other occasions when he'd written, "In the shadow of your wings I find protection until the raging storms are over" (Ps. 57:1 TEV).

All of these allusions to a safe place come alive when one is caught up in the maelstrom of a day's events where there is a sense of vulnerability and defenselessness.

"There are times when I feel like an unprotected goalie in a hockey game," a friend told me. "More pucks coming at me than I can handle: decisions to make, criticisms to respond to, problems to solve, conflicts to resolve. My stomach knots up, and I find myself breathing hard. Frankly, I just get scared. I'm not supposed to admit that I get scared, but I do nevertheless."

My friend needed a safe place, a covering like the wings of a bird. It was time to close the door, take the phone off the hook, and declare the space a safe place while the protective wings of God brought reassurance to the inner spirit. Regular occasions such as this throughout a day not

144

only prevent weariness but also replace fear with a confidence that permits the song of joy.

4. The Strong Hands

As we've already noted, it is likely that Psalm 63 was written in the context of a humiliating defeat. And, therefore, one of the issues any person in David's position is going to wrestle with is the matter of personal confidence. For in moments like these, any human-oriented confidence is probably gone.

Confidence is a state of mind and heart that permits a person to act with assurance that yesterday's defeat or failure will turn into tomorrow's victory. Real confidence is not merely a psychic energy created on a base of unfounded hopes. It is a sense of a new source of power from beyond ourselves—a power, a passion if you please, which has proved itself before and which is available to us as Christians in unlimited amounts.

We have all seen examples of people trying to build up false confidence: the boxer who makes preposterous claims before his match, the salesperson who deals in exaggerated tales about a product, the loud-mouthed adolescent who feigns bravado to cover up a load of insecurity.

But a defenseless child walking beside his or her father, held by a strong hand, is another story. This is the picture of one who assumes that his strength is an extension of the father's power. The connection of the hands makes the difference between confidence and fear.

"My soul clings to thee," David wrote, "thy right hand upholds me" (Ps. 63:8 RSV). From somewhere the king had imagined one more kind of safe place: the grip of a powerful hand offering transfused inner strength and direction.

145

I have a special memory of a day with my father on the ski slopes. It was my first time on skis, and I was as awkward and clumsy as any beginner. We rode together on the ski tow to the top of the novice's slope. And when we had positioned ourselves at the brow of the hill, I began to have second thoughts. I could hardly stand up, let alone begin any sort of glide toward the bottom.

But my father had skied the mountains for years; he had confidence, and I had trust. He drew me between his skis so that my two were inside and parallel to his. Then he put his hands on my small shoulders and pressed my body against his. "Relax," he said, "and let me guide us down the hill. You concentrate on feeling the way my body turns and makes us move from one side to the other."

It was hard at first, but I soon learned that his hands could direct me in any direction he wanted me to go. All I had to do was relax in the grasp of his hands. We actually made it to the bottom without falling, a thrilling first run. By the third time down the hill, I could almost anticipate the shift of his weight and the turning of his skis. But what I wasn't aware of at first was that the grip of his hands was becoming lighter and lighter until it was merely the light touch of his fingers.

Suddenly, the grip was no more; my dad was releasing me and permitting me to ski ahead a foot or two, reaching out to steady me only when I began to wobble. "Go ahead, son," he said halfway down the hill. "You're skiing by yourself." And I continued the descent on my own, always on the edge of losing my confidence, but nevertheless just confident enough because I could sense his strong hands just behind should I begin to fall.

Those moments in the grasp of my father's strong hands are among the most precious of my childhood memories.

146

They were there as long as I needed a transfusion of guidance and direction; they dropped away as soon as I had developed enough of my own.

The grasp of the Father's hands was a safe place to David. Like a frightened child devoid of any confidence, he reached out the imagined hands of his soul to the outstretched hand of God. Perhaps he too could visualize such an act because in his childhood he had experienced the touch of Jesse's hand at a dangerous moment. That sense of safety then became larger when he relaxed in God's hands.

Many of us were taught to act confidently even if we didn't feel confident. "Act like a man," a small boy with a bleeding knee is told. It means don't cry; don't admit that your heart is breaking and your knee hurts a lot. "Don't be such a sissy," we have heard more than once. And from words like these we learned that one should pretend that fear isn't real, that hurt shouldn't be acknowledged, that failure is a sign of weakness.

In such unfortunate ways we were denied an appreciation of the safe place. We learned to manufacture a false sense of confidence and bravery. We mastered the outward appearance of happiness even though we were crying within. We developed techniques to conceal our insecurities, techniques such as speaking boastfully, laughing heartily, and taking risks. But often, then and now, younger *or* older, we were and are just heartbroken children who refuse to let anyone decode our real language. What we usually need is the strong hand of a Father—now the heavenly Father—who says to us, "My confidence is yours. Relax, lean on me."

Why can't we stop frequently in a bone-tiring day and declare the place in which we find ourselves a safe place? In that quiet moment or hour we extend our inner spirit as a

147

child does his or her hand, and we meditate on the confidence that comes from the grip of the Holy Spirit. Frequent moments like these reinforce the promise of the Father who said, "I will uphold you with my victorious right hand" (Isa. 41:10 RSV).

In this sense the promise is reminiscent of the voice of my dad on the ski slope: "Go ahead, son." And I do because I am sure that his hands are just behind me when I will once again need a strong grip.

It is in these kinds of safe places that we hear the secrets God whispers to the inner spirit. The desert became a safe place in which Elijah could dispel the weariness of a drained condition. There he heard the still small voice of God as David might have heard it in the night hours in his sleeping room. The shoreline where Jesus cooked an early morning breakfast for the tired disciples became a safe place for the defeated Simon Peter who must have wondered whether he would ever get a second chance.

Where are your safe places and mine? Sir William Osler met a lonely child and established a safe place where she could share a confidence-building secret. Where is it that God can meet us and share His secrets?

I speak of the secrets of His power and glory, the affirmations of His steadfast love, the promises of His willingness to help when we are at wit's end, the offer of parent-like protection, the extension of His strong hand of stability and guidance.

As my life has increased in busyness and responsibility, I have found that the urgency for establishing personal and corporate safe places where these assurances can be renewed has significantly increased. The failure to understand this and act on it leads to the onset of numbing weariness and the loss of spiritual passion.

Thus I have established a safe place in my home where I pursue an encounter with God each morning. For me it is my study; for others it could be a bedroom, a kitchen, or a corner in the basement. It must be a place away from other people and varying interferences as much as possible.

Other versions of the safe place can be realized. Some of us will find them where we work or at other localities within the circumference of our daily journeys.

Occasionally we need to enter the safe places set aside by the Christian community for all to use. Those of us who have lived in the freer Protestant traditions have not been adequately taught the value of the holy places: sites exclusively reserved for worship and spiritual listening. Hearing only of the dangers of excessive emphasis upon religious architecture, we have denied ourselves the peaceful atmospheres of altars, shrines, and chapels. However legitimate the reasons for concerns about these things, insufficient thought has been given to what takes their place as an alternative.

How important it is to understand that safe places can be those where all the senses are involved in lifting us to heaven and into the presence of the waiting Father. A safe place is a place of silence where the inward ears can hear, a place of beauty where the eyes can take in color, form, and order (the symbols of God's being and actions), and a place of peace where the body can relax as the inward person reaches upward to hear the Spirit speak.

The world constructs its places of amusement, of imprisonment, of violence, and of material consumption. Why should we not be just as diligent in the development of safe places where there is the promise of peace and restoration of spiritual energy?

We must come to see that genius is involved in setting

149

aside on the maps of our lives places reserved only for the restoration of spiritual passion. We do not appreciate how much we lose by trying to renew our passion in spaces used for other things. Whenever possible, sanctuaries should not be treated as public auditoriums. And chapels should be set aside for more than occasional weddings.

Some years ago I spent a couple of weeks among a group of South American Indians to whom the gospel of Christ was a relatively new experience. At first they had chosen to worship in their community hut, the place where all the business and the conversations of the tribe took place.

But one day the missionaries were surprised by the visit of the tribal chief, who was also the pastor. "We are not pleased with worshiping God in the community hut. We think that God should be met in a special hut built only for that purpose."

I think the Indians knew something that many modern American Christians do not understand. In their desperate desire to get the church into the marketplace, some have thought it wise to combine the safe place of corporate worship with utilitarian areas for secular activities. When necessary, this is acceptable. But it is not ideal. It is highly beneficial, although not essential, to have quiet places where the secrets of the Father are shared.

Basil Pennington wrote:

We in the West are not so sensitively aware of vibrations. Yet they inevitably take their toll on us. A room that has been very full of busy activity or loud, hard music carries its charge long after. It is well to be aware of this when we have a choice of places to meditate (Pennington, *Centering Prayer*, p. 67).

We should urge upon our churches, when necessary, a

greater respect for the sanctuary as a safe place so that followers of the Lord are free to come to kneel and bow down when there is a need for the protective wing or the strong hand.

When the congregation I once served as a pastor built a new sanctuary, many of us found ourselves disliking it after our initial experience of worship in it. Why? The acoustics were different; people sat in different places during worship; a strangeness seemed to pervade the atmosphere. The feelings of God's presence were not so strong as they had been in the former place. As a worship leader, I found myself with a sense of emptiness after each Sunday morning.

We wondered what had happened. Had we made a colossal mistake? Then we realized that a sanctuary, a safe place, is only part architecture and structure; the rest comprises memories and experiences with God. Our new safe place needed some time in which to store the memories of the special times when God had met us.

My wife, Gail, uses an old black frying pan when she wants to make the best pancakes. "The secret of this pan," she told me, "is in the buildup of grease from all the times I've used it." The buildup she called it.

Special safe places get better and better because of the buildup. Our new sanctuary needed a buildup of memories: memories of God's comfort when we were grieving, of God's blessing when someone got married, of God's majesty when we had profound experiences of worship, of God's redeeming mercy when various individuals found Christ in conversion, of God's forgiveness when people shook off spiritual coldness and recommitted themselves to following Christ. Then a new auditorium became a sanctuary, a safe place to which we all love to come.

Not only can we create safe places in our homes and in

151

our sanctuaries, but we can occasionally go to other places where spiritual discipline and activity are encouraged.

The retreat movement across the country is advancing with exciting speed because busy people are discovering safe places away from the relentless noises and intrusions of modern society.

Our Roman Catholic friends have known this for centuries. And the good news is that many Protestant churches and organizations are realizing the value of maintaining places where hurting, confused, or spiritually-disoriented men and women can go to find peace and renewal for a short time. But the remedial purposes are not the only ones. Many of us should consider retreats to *avoid* confusion and exhaustion.

Throughout the day, one should not be reluctant to create momentary safe places: at the desk, in the car, on public transportation, in a waiting room. They are not the best of places, but they can work.

These moments of sanctuary become mini-versions of what Abraham did in the countryside when he stopped his traveling and built an altar to his God. "This is a safe place," he declared by constructing the altar. And there God came and spoke to him. So we too build altars in our hearts just as David built in his a sanctuary on the desert.

The first recorded martyr of the Christian church was Stephen. Because he spoke boldly before his fellow Jews, he was dragged beyond the city walls to a place of execution. The rocks began to fall upon his body, and soon he was dying. It is important to note what Stephen did as he lay there feeling the terrible blows of the stones crashing upon him. He created a safe place, and he cried out, "Lord Jesus, receive my spirit." And kneeling down, he cried out, "Lord do not hold this sin against them" (Acts 7:59,60 RSV).

Luke, the writer, continued, "And when he had said this, he fell asleep" (Acts 7:60 RSV). Stephen's declared safe place became a resting place. A map of his life journey will show that ugly spot as a place of violence for his persecutors. But the map will also show it as a safe place for Stephen. If there is such a map of my life, where might it show the safe places I have established? That is a piercing question

14

The Still Times

The asphalt road on which we drive the last few miles to Peace Ledge, our New Hampshire retreat, is beautiful in the fall. In the early spring, however, the road looks like a disaster area. FROST HEAVES, a sign explains to drivers in late March as the ground begins to thaw on warm days.

Each day the road seems to buckle more and more until it has the properties of an old washboard. Here and there potholes open up where water has seeped in and frozen in the night air. The car tires beat the road surface into chunks, and before long the entire length of Shaker Road is a mess.

It occurred to me one day that while Shaker Road was like that in the early spring, the connecting State Route 106 wasn't. In fact it was as smooth as glass, a pleasure to drive, spring or fall. What made the difference between the two?

The road repair gang gave me the simple explanation one day. When Route 106 had been constructed, the work crew had carefully laid a thick bed of gravel beneath the roadbed that provided the necessary drainage. The roadbed was deep enough that it was untouched by the cold going into the ground or the frost coming out of it.

154

Not so with the Shaker Road, the men told me. There, the ground had simply been graded and a thick patch of asphalt laid over it. "A quick and dirty job," someone said.

With an inadequate bed, the road was torn up every spring by the moisture underneath that worked into every crack and made the subsurface unreliable. The auto and truck tires did the rest.

How important it is, I thought as I compared the two kinds of roads, to make sure that my public life does not have the marks of a Shaker-Road construction. If I do not give attention to the subsurface, the cracks and strains will quickly show the minute the surface changes or stresses occur.

How important it is for me to give careful attention to the subsurface, my inner spirit, making sure it is strong enough and properly maintained so that it can support the stress of the real world.

That's when I began to think about the *rest* component in my life. For in proper rest I am tending to the subsurface upon which the road of daily living is laid. I say *proper rest* because much of what we call rest today is merely amusement or leisure, a temporary patch over weariness. It has about the same value as the quick hot patches the road crew puts over holes and ridges on Shaker Road. Their job makes for smooth driving for about three days, and then it's back to the washboard again.

The only answer to a "washboardy" road is to tear it up and treat the roadbed to a deep thickness of drainage material. The only answer to an exhausted, passionless life is to check the condition of the subsurface, the inner spirit. That's where Sabbath, the *still time*, comes in.

When I wrote of Sabbath in the book *Ordering Your Private World*, I was impressed with the number of people

155

who sent letters to me, responding with curiosity and fascination on that subject. Often they spoke of their frustration with an enlarging schedule, of events and commitments seemingly out of control, of calendars jammed with good things to do. Did I really believe, many asked, that the Sabbath principle was the answer to the problem or the prevention of exhaustion? Yes, I answered, in many cases; perhaps it is not the entire answer, but it is a major step in the right direction.

As I write this chapter, I am in Brazil where I have been giving a series of talks to missionaries. On this very day, one of the men stopped to talk with me about his fellow workers. "They have so much to do," he said, "and they are absolutely spent. I see them going about from one task to another almost as if they are in a daze. There is a joylessness in what they are doing. I fear that many of them are on the edge of a dreadful burnout."

I asked him when he and his colleagues stopped their work. "They never do, really," he replied. "We seem to goad each other on actually. You see, it wouldn't be good to be playing or relaxing when another missionary stopped by on business and found us doing something that wasn't serious. I'm afraid we have a way of making one another feel quite small when we catch each other napping. We don't have to say anything; the other knows he's been caught. So if we stop working, we do it on the sly; we don't let anyone know about it. Which means we are ashamed of rest."

Is rest not considered a "serious" thing? I wondered aloud. Do we think of time away from work as a waste, as a second-class hour? That certainly doesn't reflect a biblical view of things.

Sabbath is God's antidote to workaholism. It is the checkmate to men and women who have fallen into the trap of believing that their personal worth is built upon what they do rather than what they are. I like the word *Sabbath*; it falls into the same family of words from which we get *rest* and *peace*. In the larger sense it has the notion of things being in proper order, like the balls racked inside the form on the pool table.

I like to refer to Sabbath as the still time, the special moment in my calendar. If the map of my life should be marked with frequent safe places, the calendar of my life should show sabbaths or still times. These are the moments (or hours) when we say to the noise and turmoil of the schedule just what Jesus said to a storm that seemed to be threatening the life of His disciples: "Peace! Be still!" (Mark 4:39 RSV). Instantly, a raging lake became a safe place in a still time.

SEVEN PRINCIPLES OF STILL TIMES THAT RENEW SPIRITUAL PASSION

Just as I must regularly assume control over places and say, "This is a safe place," so must I wrest away control of my time and say, "This is a still time. Accordingly, I press peace and rest into the calendar."

The Role-Model Principle

God has taught us the special principle of *still time* in a number of ways. He taught it by modeling it in His own self-revelation.

There is a still time inferred at the conclusion of each of the days of creation. "And God said . . ." refers to the work God gave Himself to do. "And God saw . . ." refers to the still moments at the end of the work in which God stamped value and closure on what he had done. "And God saw that it was good" (Gen. 1:18 RSV).

157

It would appear that God our Creator never engaged in a succeeding phase of work before He had brought to conclusion the previous phase by a "Sabbathing" moment, a still time in which value was assigned to the creative labor.

Then when the entire week of creation labor was complete, there was a major still time as the entire project was studied and valued.

"A work unexamined by a superior is valueless," a close and admired friend told me as he talked about the practice of responsible management. Who could examine God's work except God? The fact that the Bible records that He appraised His own work and placed value upon it is very significant. Why mention the matter at all? Because it is to be a precedent and an example for us.

The Rhythm Principle

The writer of Genesis said:

> By the seventh day God had finished the work he had been doing; so on the seventh day he rested from all his work. And God blessed the seventh day and made it holy, because on it he rested from all the work of creating that he had done" (Gen. 2:2,3 NIV).

This remarkable rhythm in the work of God ought not to be taken lightly. Combined with the rhythms of rest we see in almost all of nature, it provides us with a stunning lesson on the importance of true rest—not merely the rest of the body but also the rest of the spirit. The heart, probably the strongest and most resilient of our muscles, is designed to be still between every beat. Most growing things observe a period of dormancy every year. Every cycle is completed by a period of stillness.

It is said of one of the famous composers that he had a rebellious son who used to come in late at night after his father and mother had gone to bed. And before going to his own room, he would go to his father's piano and slowly, as well as loudly, play a simple scale, all but the final note. Then leaving the scale uncompleted, he would retire to his room. Meanwhile the father, hearing the scale minus the final note, would writhe on his bed, his mind unable to relax because the scale was unresolved. Finally, in consternation, he would stumble down the stairs and hit the previously unstruck note. Only then would his mind surrender to sleep once again.

God's labor seems never to be complete until, like the final note on the scale, the concluding still time, a pause that looks backward and pronounces completion and value.

After the creation account of God's own still times, we do not come again to the Sabbath principle until Exodus 16 when the chosen people were well on their way from Egypt toward Mount Sinai. Food had become an issue: how would they eat? where was the sustenance going to come from?

God will provide, Moses informed the people. Every morning you will go out of your tents, and you will find manna, a strange kind of nourishment, on the ground. You can gather just enough for you and your family. Save more than that, and it will spoil on you.

In such a way the God of Israel was teaching his people about a new and healthier concept of work. It is important to remember that they had been slaves for almost four hundred years, their labor always at the behest of someone who owned them and ordered them into action. It is probable that they had had no control over their own time and that they had no conception of how to order their own days now that the yoke of slavery had been overthrown.

God's gifts of food were not to be hoarded and turned into wealth for those who could gather faster than others. And it was no time for one family to go into business gathering for another family, thus perpetuating the slavery all over again. But, the rules pointed toward a time of rest also.

> Each morning everyone gathered as much as he needed, and when the sun grew hot, it melted away. On the sixth day, they gathered twice as much—two omers for each person—and the leaders of the community came and reported this to Moses. He said to them, "This is what the LORD commanded: 'Tomorrow is to be a day of rest, a holy Sabbath to the LORD. So bake what you want to bake and boil what you want to boil. Save whatever is left and keep it until morning'" (Exod. 16:21–23 NIV).

Some people learned a few things the hard way. Those who had originally disobeyed Moses and gathered more than they needed during the weekdays had been surprised by maggots in their hoarded food the next morning. But this was not so for food gathered before the Sabbath.

The Rest Principle

Now perhaps there was another lesson to learn the hard way. Those who may not have seen the importance of gathering a twofold portion on the day before Sabbath learned on Sabbath morning that they were going to be hungry for a while. Nothing was going to materialize. Previously, they'd not eaten because of spoiled food. Now they could not eat because of their failure to collect food when it was available and because God insisted that work stop on the Sabbath.

In such elementary, but nevertheless effective, ways did the God of Moses teach the people that he meant business about a time of rest. If it seems that He was going about things in an extreme way, it is important to remember that this Sabbath concept was being taught to virtual children, who had not known the meaning of rest or personal discipline for centuries. You have to start somewhere, and this is how God did it. An object lesson whose consequences and rewards were extremely practical.

Thus it would not be a surprise when later Moses would appear before the same people with Ten Commandments, the irreducible minimums of behavior that would become the core principles of their life together before Him. Think of it! *Just ten!* And among the ten was a commandment speaking to the issue of the still time.

Remember the Sabbath day by keeping it holy. Six days you shall labor and do all your work, but the seventh day is a Sabbath to the LORD your God. On it you shall not do any work, neither you, nor your son or daughter, nor your manservant or maidservant, nor your animals, nor the alien within your gates. For in six days the LORD made the heavens and the earth, the sea, and all that is in them, but he rested on the seventh day. Therefore the LORD blessed the Sabbath day and made it holy (Exod. 20:8–11 NIV).

This would be the first of a number of fences God would build into the kingdom lifestyle of the chosen people. The fences, or disciplines, were important, first of all, because they provided marks of distinctiveness for those living in agreement with God's Lordship. In the case of the Sabbath day, a uniqueness of life was being demonstrated, a way to divide time.

161

I am convinced additionally that the Sabbath was a necessary discipline protecting against what we would later call workaholism, the tendency to use time flagrantly in the building of one's fortune at the expense of a more balanced and spiritually oriented life. This would not be the only place such a discipline would check the tendency toward excessive living.

If the Sabbath was a hedge against workaholism, forcing an interruption to the workweek, the tithe (the giving of the first and the best of a person's productivity) would be a bar against materialism. It is virtually impossible for a person to become an obsessive hoarder of material things when the tithe is built in as a discipline. In those areas most likely to dominate a life to excess—workaholism and materialism—working principles prevent people from destroying themselves by imbalanced living.

The Sabbath, the still time, began as a law. It is my conviction that it would later become a principle of time budgeting. By principle rather than by law, I am suggesting that the Sabbath, become less a legal requirement—one day per week—and more a principle of rest that should be observed by the mature person on many, many occasions, perhaps even several times per day.

My friends in Orthodox Judaism and those whom I know in the Seventh Day Adventist tradition strongly reject this idea, believing the Sabbath can never be seen in any light other than that of a law about a specific span of time, and they have my admiration and respect.

But I am convinced that what begins as law in the life of a child (the first-generation Hebrews) becomes principle in the life of an adult (we who are the inheritors of centuries of teaching and experience). The principle of Sabbath should be an even more healthy perspective than the law of Sabbath if we understand its purpose and commit to observing it with frequency.

The Remembrance Principle

What were the components of the legal Sabbath that God taught to Israel? First, *remember!* In the Hebrew world it was a dynamic action when one remembered. The effort was that of attempting to fully experience a previous event as if it were happening all over again.

In this case the event is specifically the seventh day of creation when God rested. Thus to remember is to rest from labor as God rested. It is to look back over the work and appraise it as God appraised His work.

To keep the day holy meant that it should be set apart and treated unlike any other parcel of time during the week. This still time was to be absolutely unique from any other time: a different set of activities, a different kind of thinking.

The Renunciation Principle

When Moses first set forth the Sabbath concept as part of the law, an important component of what he was saying had to do with the concept of renunciation, the renunciation of work—not because work is a bad thing, but because if it is not contained, it gets out of control and captures the affections of the worker, causing work to lose its meaning and leaving no time for worship or rest. Moses was telling the people that a good thing must be renounced because a better thing must take precedence for a short while.

The law also indicates how strongly this renunciation was meant to be. The *entire household* had to renounce

163

work. Little would have been accomplished if the house-holder had merely remanded the regular workload to his servants and hirelings. Then he could have enjoyed the fruits of the work without any exertion himself. No! The entire community had to stop and enter into still time.

The Refreshment Principle

In later amplifications on the Sabbath matter, Moses is even more explicit. In Exodus 31, for example, he told the people that the day was not only holy to God but holy *for* them. I hear him telling the people that everyone profits from this sort of rest-rhythm. And for what purposes?

First, it was a sign of the special relationship between the nation and the Lord. But, second, it brings a kind of re-freshment. "And God rested and refreshed himself" is the literal wording of verse 17.

How can God be in need of refreshment since he never exhausts Himself? That is hard to answer except to say that if God reveals Himself and refreshes Himself, it is in part because He wants to point out to us the importance of our refreshing ourselves.

And that fact simply isn't going over too well with many Christian people today—either because they struggle to know what genuine rest is or because they have filled their lives with so many things to do that Sabbath rest has been squeezed out and put in the discretionary column. Such action means, of course, that Sabbath rest will rarely be seen, if at all.

The first of the struggles, a knowledge of real rest, is a great one, because leisure and amusement have so com-pletely covered up our concept of genuine rest. Although a

164

certain release and relaxation accompany most forms of leisure and amusement, I think it is safe to say that the real deep-seated exhaustion, that of the spirit, is hardly touched at all.

Modern play is good, of course, for building relationships, for exercising the body, and for stimulating the mind. But this play may not reach down to the lowest layers of our real weariness, where the inner spirit takes the battering of spiritual warfare.

The awareness that we need to give attention to the resting of our spirits is almost nonexistent. What the early saints knew so well about taking time each day in the Sabbath tradition for the recollecting of the spirit has been reduced in modern times to something called the "quiet time," neglected by most and overorganized by many others—neglected because quiet time usually brings so little sense of value; overorganized because it falls victim to those who typically think that everything is best reduced to a method even if it does destroy spontaneity or, ironically, the ability of the Spirit of God to speak to us.

Need I say more about the second struggle, that of simply crowding Sabbath out of the calendar altogether? As I have often observed, being too busy has been so very easy for many of us, including myself. I am an action person. I prefer motion to stillness, noise to silence, and initiation to passivity. Thus, when instant choices have to be made about what is the best use of any period of time, those of us engaged in busyness are most likely to decide on apparent productive activity rather than on quiet and reflective activity. That kind of thinking is the culture's "gift" to us.

My friend Margaret Jensen in her lovely book about a friend, Lena, tells of a moment when the two spoke of the meaning of rest and our struggle to accept it as part of life. Lena said,

God rested on the seventh day. He just finished creating everything. If that had been you and me, most likely we would have organized all we did those six days. Sometimes God says, "Sit down, child. Take the weight off your feet and start believing in your heart" (Jensen, *Lena,* p. 64).

I am convinced that every one of us who has chosen to follow after Christ must take this still-time discipline seriously. Not to do it is to violate a principle of life taught to the people of Israel. And not to do it is to strangle our inner spirit to the point of inaction—weariness of the worst kind.

The Recurrence Principle

I am also convinced that Sabbath, the recollection of the spirit, is more than just a day in our time. It is a recurring event throughout each of our days. Just as a safe place can be more than a sanctuary, a Sabbath can be more than a day each week. Sabbaths can be short bursts of spiritual recollecting, reminding me of the quick pitstops of the Indianapolis racer when there is a need for fuel, tires, and refreshment. (But of course, I would hope that our Sabbath pauses are not as frantic as the Indianapolis pitstops.)

François Fénelon wrote to a friend in need of spiritual instruction:

You must learn . . . to make good use of chance moments, when waiting for someone, when going from place to place, or when in society where to be a good listener is all that is required; . . . at such times it is easy to lift the heart to God, and thereby gain fresh strength for further duties. The less time one has the more carefully it should be managed. If you wait for free, convenient seasons in which to fulfill real duties, you run the risk of waiting forever; especially in such a life as yours. No, make use of chance moments (Fénelon, *Spiritual Letters to Women*, p. 16).

Busy people like young mothers will be comforted by Fenelon's words because his "short snatches" are all they have for several years when their children are small and weariness from sleepless nights are a regularity. The key, of course, is to snatch something.

Ruth Graham has shared many times that she used to leave books open all over the house so that when a chance offered itself for her to get a moment or two of reading and meditation, she could reach for the nearest ready volume. To "create the Sabbathing moment," even if it is a terribly brief one, is an all-important pursuit whether we're talking about mothers or businesspeople or students. One thought in such a pause can be the big difference in how the next hours are going to be lived, whether they will be in spiritual passion or in drudgery.

God is not desirous of making us feel guilty when extended periods of silence and worship are impossible. He would prefer, I believe, that we be prodded toward Sabbaths by a spiritual homesickness for His renewal presence. There's a great difference between the two motivating forces. If we discover the habit of snatching Sabbath moments, we will be pressing God's presence into the day, something like holes in a piece of Swiss cheese.

So it is that the frost heaves of personal life are confronted and smoothed out. By laying an adequate roadbed in the inner spirit, we can prevent the hostile elements that cause fatigue. And that happens only when Sabbaths find their way into the calendars of our lives: monthly, weekly, daily, hourly.

15
Special Friends

In Joseph Heller's novel *Something Happened*, the fictional narrator, Bob Slocum, describes the nature of human relationships among the people in the company for which he has worked for almost twenty years. It is a bleak description of tired and directionless men and women. The overarching theme lacing those relationships together, Slocum indicates, is fear. Of his peers and subordinates, he says:

> In my department, there are six people who are afraid of me, and one small secretary who is afraid of all of us. I have one other person working for me who is not afraid of anyone, not even me. . . .
>
> The thought occurs to me often that there must be mail clerks, office boys and girls, stock boys, messengers, and assistants of all kinds and ages who are afraid of everyone in the company (Heller, *Something Happened*, p. 12).

Bob Slocum is even more descriptive of his relationship to his boss, Jack Green.

> Often, I protect and defend [Jack Green] when he is late or forgetful with work of his own, and I frequently give

him credit for good work from my department that he does not deserve. But I never tell him I do this; and I never let him know when I hear anything favorable about him. I enjoy seeing Green apprehensive. I'm pleased he distrusts me (it does wonders for my self-esteem), and I do no more than necessary to reassure him.

And I am the best friend he has here (pp. 27).

Slocum describes an exhausting work environment. This is a place where people are drained of productive and creative energy because they spend so much time wondering whether a "teammate" is really a competitor. People get weary in a place like that.

I strongly suspect that many people we know work in similar situations. Perhaps even more people might admit, if asked, that their family lives are marked with this unfortunate kind of interpersonal play. Would yet another group suggest that their church experiences are characterized by similar dynamics?

When you see a cluster of people who drain each other in this fashion, mentally picture a stretched tandem bicycle where three people are supposed to be peddling. Most of us have seen the humorous vignette, usually in cartoon form, in which only the first person peddles strenuously while the second and third become passengers who sit back and enjoy the view. The first never looks around to see what the other two are doing. He assumes that they are working as hard as he is. But they're not, and one is left to do the work of three, spending most of his energy just to keep the bicycle upright and in motion rather than going somewhere. Therefore, weariness sets in, a slow and certain loss of desire to keep on going.

The opposite picture of Joseph Heller's fear-filled office

staff is that of Moses on a hilltop in the book of Exodus. He and his people had encountered the hostile Amalek who would not permit them to pass through the land on their way to Mount Sinai. It was the first serious crisis in the life of the chosen people since they had crossed the Red Sea.

Moses won because he operated from relational strength as he faced the battle. His battle plan depended upon relationships, the kind I'll eventually call special friends.

"Choose for us men, and go out and fight with Amalek," he said to Joshua. "Tomorrow I will stand on the top of the hill with the rod of God in my hand" (Exod. 17:9 RSV). So Joshua went with the army of Israel to the valley to face Amalek, and Moses went with his aides, Aaron and Hur, to the mountaintop to hold the rod, symbolizing God's power and authority.

It was an interesting day of ups and downs as one army and then the other prevailed in battle. The Scripture says that whenever Moses held his hands with the rod upward, the armies of Israel began to advance against Amalek. But when he dropped his arms, the battle turned against the Israelites.

"But Moses' hands grew weary," the writer noted. And that was the cue for his aides to move into action. Finding a stone for Moses to sit on, Aaron and Hur stood on each side and held up his arms "so that his hands were steady until the going down of the sun" (v. 12).

Down in the valley, "Joshua mowed down Amalek and his people" (v. 13). Strange circumstances; uncommon strategies. But the underlying message is timeless. A man was surrounded with what I want to call *special friends*, and together *they accomplished what no one of them could have done alone*.

If each of us has a map in our lives showing our safe places and a calendar showing our still times, then we also should have an address book that lists our special friends. Who are they?

Special friends. Moses' address book would have included *Joshua*, the man in the valley coordinating the effort as well as *Aaron* and *Hur*, the men on each side holding Moses' arms heavenward "so that his hands were steady." What weariness would have made impossible if Moses had insisted on performing alone, the help of special friends made triumphant. Clearly a team.

Special friends are part of the economy of spiritual passion, and in most cases an indispensable part. Unlike the very draining and the very nice people of our worlds, special friends are committed to helping one another discover and maintain spiritual passion. Each member of a team of special friends rejoices when another succeeds. Each weeps when another falls. Special friends do not envy when someone wins; nor do they gloat at failure.

In recent years there has been a welcomed revolution in our understanding of Christian relationships. We have a superabundance of books on marriage, family, and the healing of the hurting. And this revolution has affected our consciousness in building strong personal relationships. Perhaps not enough has been written, however, from a proactive perspective on relationships—that is, from a continuing value placed on the team and teamwork. I'm speaking of the way we enter into fellowship with one another in order to enhance and protect each other's potential or vulnerabilities.

A recent novel and movie featured a young U.S. Air Force fighter pilot who struggles against the concept of teamwork. As the story develops, it becomes clear that the pilot's peers in the fighter squadron easily agree that he is the best pilot in the Air Force . . . but, they always add, also the most dangerous. He regularly breaks the basic rules of flying protocol; he flies his planes to the outermost limits of stress; and he ruthlessly competes to win every inter-squadron flying contest.

In spite of the fact that he is the best, no one wants him around. Why? Because others have learned that he cares for no one but himself. He is incapable of being part of a team of special friends.

The story line highlights the struggle of an individualist who will ultimately accomplish nothing if he cannot become a team player. Refusing to obey orders, he abandons a fellow flyer in the midst of a simulated aerial battle and the other pilot is shot down. Unwilling to accept the stress limits of his plane, he crashes himself and his navigator dies in the accident. Only then does the horror of the consequences of his lone-ranger performance begin to settle deep within. By the conclusion of the story, the young man has begun to understand the meaning of special friends who lift one another to even greater personal achievement.

May I emphasize that I am saying special *friends* and not *acquaintances.* For it is the latter that most of us have; not the former. Our busy lives and calendars make little room for special friends. In order to have them, one must invest prime time to cultivate and maintain them, time that might have to be taken from other good goals and objectives.

Most of us would be tempted to think that cultivating special friends is something done over and above our work. I have come to believe that the developing special friends is *part* of our work.

The apostle Paul was clearly a man committed to raising up a band of special friends. He knew who they were, and he regularly recognized them for their contribution to his spiritual passion. His friends were a resource upon which he obviously depended and without which he would not have survived.

His address book of special friends would have included Acquilla and Priscilla with whom he occasionally worked and lived (see Acts 18:3), Onesiphorus ("for he oft refreshed me" 2 Tim. 1:16 KJV), Philemon ("I have derived much joy and comfort from your love" Philem. 1:7 RSV), Luke, and a host of others. Paul's friends came in all ages and backgrounds, and he seems to have taken great care to cultivate them.

God "comforted us," he wrote when describing his own numbing weariness, "by the coming of Titus" (2 Cor. 7:6 RSV). On the terribly tiring trip to Rome, there was a moment when the brethren from the church heard that Paul was not far from his destination.

And the brethren there, when they heard of us, came as far as the Forum of Appius and Three Taverns to meet us. *On seeing them Paul thanked God and took courage.* (Acts 28:15 RSV, emphasis added).

We are reading about a cadre of special friends in motion, and when they came, they brought the possibility of the restoration of Paul's spiritual passion, much of which had probably been drained away in the exhaustion of travel. Quite different, wouldn't you say, from the office climate of Joseph Heller's novel?

Who are the special friends, the teammates in our address books? Our special friends are the men and women for whom the subject of spiritual passion is an important item. I have pondered this question recently with great seriousness. And perhaps the question is an important one

173

which men (*particularly* men) ask in their midlife years.

Recently I had the opportunity to sit for several hours with a group of brilliant and very successful engineers and executives and to talk with them about spiritual and personal disciplines. At no time during the day did the group show greater interest in what I had come to say when we began to talk about special friends.

"It is not uncommon for middle-life men to discover that they are very lonely," I had said. "If you ask them who their close friends are, most will say, 'I don't think I have any close friends.'"

The group wanted to talk about why that was true for so many of them. Why had they lost the ability to make such friendships? And why did most of them look back at their college days as the last time when there had been that sort of intimacy?

The probable answer? I proposed to them that middle-life men have probably spent so much of their energies establishing themselves as functional successes in their careers that they had not taken the time to think about relational success. Then at the "noon of life," as Carl Jung once called it, they realize they have not attained adequate intimacy with their spouses and children, who are now probably passing into adolescence. What's more, they have lost contact with almost all intimate friends from school days, leaving only their working associates.

As I talked of these things, it became clear that this matter of special friends was a serious issue with these men, and we spent a significant amount of time talking about how to regain the momentum of special-friend building.

What are the component parts of the special friend resource? I am thinking of the kind of teammates we need. Some of us are just old enough to remember the old corner-lot baseball games. Garbage can lids served as bases; lines hastily toed into the ground served as foul-ball indicators. And the teams were divvied up by two captains who threw a bat back and forth to determine who got first choice. The alternative choices of the captains were determined by who could play what position. The important thing, if you were captain, was knowing what kind of teammates you needed to complement your own strengths.

SIX SPECIAL-FRIEND TEAMMATES THAT HELP YOU MAINTAIN SPIRITUAL PASSION

Let's think through the sort of team capable of providing spiritual passion for each of its players. What kind of players and positions are necessary to the objective? There are several positions, if you please, and I doubt that any one person could ever fulfill (or should fulfill) all of these parts. But what is important is that the man or woman wanting to maintain and develop spiritual passion should take an inventory of personal relationships to see if these special-friend teammates are there. For if they are not, we may find ourselves the front rider on the tandem bike, pedaling more weight than our own and wondering why we are not making more headway. Let me list a few special-friend teammates.

1. The Sponsor

Students of the life of President Dwight David Eisenhower generally agree that his military career in the U.S. Army was colorless and devoid of recognition until he was transferred to the Panama Canal Zone, where he served for several years under the command of General Fox Connor. A special relationship between the two developed, and Connor became Eisenhower's *sponsor*. The result? Eisenhower suddenly began to show the leadership and organizational qualities that ultimately brought him to the notice of General George Marshall, who appointed him to lead the armies that invaded Europe in World War II. Looking back on that special-friend relationship with Fox Connor, Eisenhower later wrote:

> Life with General Connor was a sort of graduate school in military affairs and the humanities, leavened by a man who was experienced in his knowledge of men and their conduct. I can never adequately express my gratitude to this one gentleman. . . . In a lifetime of association with great and good men, he is the one more or less invisible figure to whom I owe an incalculable debt (Eisenhower, *At Ease*, p. 136)

Those comments suggest why I'd call Fox Connor a sponsor. The sponsor, of course, is another name for mentor or discipler. We have already looked at the role of the sponsor in another context when we thought about VRP's, the very resourceful people who pour energy or passion into us rather than drain it away.

But let's take a second look at this role now in the context of the special-friend team. The sponsor is that Very Resourceful Person (the VRP) who ushers us into opportunity and possibility. He or she is usually close by and can be drawn upon when courage, guidance, or assurance is needed that a path chosen is the right one.

Few examples of the sponsor relationship are better than the one between Mordecai and Esther in the Old Testament. The Jews in Babylon had been threatened by a holocaust through the manipulations of Haman, a close counselor to the king. For a while it appeared as if nothing

176

could be done to set aside the edict the king had signed, apparently in ignorance of its implications (see Esther 3:7–12).

Parallel to these events, the king had brought into his palace a new wife, Esther, chosen as far as we can tell for her remarkable beauty. As was the custom in those days, Esther could come into the presence of the king only when she was invited (see Esther 4:11). To do otherwise was to call down upon herself the sentence of death.

It was Mordecai who was Esther's sponsor. A close relative, he had raised her from childhood. And in the midst of the crisis he sent a message asking if she would approach the king and appeal the matter of Haman's edict and the Jewish predicament. Her first response to her sponsor was negative because of the rules. And Mordecai responded:

> "Think not that in the king's palace you will escape any more than all the other Jews. For if you keep silence at such a time as this, relief and deliverance will rise for the Jews from another quarter, but you and your father's house will perish. And who knows whether you have not come to the kingdom for such a time as this?" (Esther 4:13–14).

With this sort of urging, Esther changed her mind and sprang into action, and it eventuated in the saving of the entire Jewish population in the empire.

But how had it happened? Was it Esther's own passion that did the job? Not by any stretch of the imagination. Alone she would have been paralyzed in inaction. No, the passion came through performance of a sponsor. You could say that Esther had a special friend, one who urged her on, convinced her that this was her responsibility, her opportunity. He literally seems to have pressed courage into her, and he did it merely through a written message.

Such was the extent of Mordecai's influence on the young woman that that was all it took, and she headed for the king's quarters (see Esther 5:1).

What had Mordecai done? He had communicated from a larger perspective outside the palace and interpreted it to Esther: the issue, the danger, the possibility, the heavenly viewpoint. Esther's situation had limited her to seeing only the restrictive customs and the personal dangers. Alone, she didn't have the slightest idea what to do. But Mordecai appreciated the potential of her position, and he called her attention to it. His was the role of the cheerleader: "You can do it!" And she did.

That is the classic role of sponsors or mentors. When they do their job, there is a whole new dimension of reality for the one who is being sponsored. Sponsors help generate spiritual passion and vision. They often convey the sense of possibility. God uses sponsors to move the Esthers into action.

My own feeling is that all of us need sponsors until we are well into midlife. Then perhaps we outgrow the need. We may not draw upon them with great frequency, but it is good to know they are there and we can draw from them in a healthy sense whenever there is a need for an Esther-like decision.

Whenever I have the chance to sit and talk with young men and women about sponsors or mentors I am inevitably asked the same question: "Where can I find a sponsor like the one you describe?" The simple answer I usually give is, "Go out and find one whose lifestyle and performance seem to fulfill what you dream of becoming."

"I have," often comes back the answer. "But when I locate someone like that, I usually find out the person is too busy."

Too busy! I suspect they're right. Contemporary life is so clogged with things to do that the sponsorship relationship is being sacrificed all too often, both by the would-be sponsor and the "sponsoree." Sponsorship takes time, more time than most people involved in programs and high-flying activities have to give. The result? The Christian community will probably lose a significant number of potential leaders who needed the kind of strength a special friend, like a sponsor, might have given.

The sponsor is not necessarily a friend. He or she enters our lives for a specific purpose and for a given period of time. There is usually an objective to the relationship: to develop a younger or more inexperienced person into something. Then, even as Christ said to his disciples at the end of almost three years, "It is to your advantage that I go away: (John 16:7 RSV).

"My sponsors tend to be dead people," I've often heard my wife, Gail, say. "I found them in the great biographies where I was able to discover the hidden secrets of great men and women of God. It's not quite the same, but it helped a lot when there were no older, more experienced people who were willing to provide me with the time I needed to grow."

Very few things would be more effective in the raising up of a powerful and passionate people to expand Christ's kingdom than the choice by mature Christians to become special-friend sponsors to younger Christians in need of models and cheerleaders.

A severe price the church is paying today is the choice of older women to return to work in the marketplace after childraising for no reason other than to make more money or to find an extra dosage of "meaning and identity in life."

Granted, some must do this for economic reasons—col-

179

lege tuition is a common reason—but one notes with concern those who have not seen the biblical injunction for the older to disciple or sponsor the younger. Is there a greater contribution to society than the gift of one's self to a younger generation? Young people cry out for sponsors, especially if they come from homes broken with relational sickness.

In my list of special-friend teammates, I would next call attention to the position of the affirmer.

2. The Affirmer

The *affirmer* has to be the second person in our address book of special friends. He or she is the one who moves alongside and inspirits us as we act out our destiny. The affirmer takes up where the sponsor leaves off. The affirmer takes note of what we are doing and what we are becoming and attaches value to it.

Nowhere is the role of the affirmer more beautifully illustrated than in the moments following the baptism of Jesus. The baptism was for sinners, for those in need of public repentance. Because he was sinless Jesus had no need of such baptism, but He chose to do it anyway, both as an example and as an identification with the people for whom He would later die.

Is there any temptation on His part as He leaves the waters to wonder what the heavenly Father thinks of what He has just done? Is there any sensation pointing up the coming agony of the cross that could cause undue fear? Could He be tempted to feel that He has diminished Himself by identifying with the sins of the human race?

If there were temptations to self-doubt, they had to have been quickly dispelled by the affirmation of the Father who

180

from Heaven said, "Thou art my beloved Son; with thee I am well pleased" (Mark 1:11 RSV). In one simple statement the solidarity of the Father/Son relationship was affirmed, the act which Jesus had gone through was positively acknowledged, and the correctness of His motivation was underscored. His spiritual passion was renewed, if indeed it had at all been diminished.

We must not mistake affirmation for the empty compliments and plaudits that are carelessly tossed about in human relationships. Affirmation is the genuine act of mutual discovery and evaluation. Affirmation is not impulsive, and it is not given with the motive of obtaining a reciprocal favor. Affirmation is one person's assistance to another so that he or she can see the life of God in action and in being.

I have worked in ministry with a number of people who were the product of a tradition that mindlessly ignored affirmation because it robbed glory from God. If that were the case, Paul robbed God of glory when he affirmed the Thessalonian congregation for becoming an example "to all the believers in Macedonia" (1 Thess. 1:7), when he affirmed Philemon for the love he had "toward all the saints" (Philem. 1:5), and when he affirmed Epaphroditus for the faithfulness of his service to Paul at the risk of his own life.

When affirmation is denied—especially among the younger of us—it leaves people struggling, wondering if their contribution is substantial, whether or not it makes a difference. Thus the resulting loss of nerve, of spiritual passion.

Like others, I have experienced both the work of the affirmer and the *de-firmer*. (I have just coined a word.)

The de-firmer works from insensitivity, ignorance, indifference, or (worse yet) plain, pure malice. The de-firmer picks the time when you have finished something that has

181

cost you spiritual, emotional, and physical energy and then questions your motives, the quality of your work, or the results you set out to achieve. Instantly, you are hurt, tempted to quit, angry and wanting to fight back. In expending your passion, you become vulnerable to even the slightest attack (remember Elijah!), and the de-firmer senses that and uses the leverage of the moment to put you down.

We not only have to be able to spot the de-firmer coming at us, but we need to ask ourselves if we too have been guilty of de-firmation on occasions. It is easy to become a de-firmer and not know it until too late.

But there are the affirming experiences also. Recently, I was preparing to preach at a well-known church in the Midwest. I was tired, wishing I was home and wondering how I'd gotten into the responsibility I was facing. You could hardly say I was spiritually impassioned to face that congregation with a word from God.

Then an usher stepped to my side and handed me a note. An anonymous writer reminded me of a recent place where I had given a series of talks and described the difference my talks had made in his life and that of his family. He included in the note a written prayer asking the Spirit of God to anoint me for the coming pulpit experience. Instantly I took on a new quantity of courage and desire. Passion came about as the result of an affirmation. I had no doubt that the notewriter, whose name was not included on the paper, was God's gift to me.

Sponsors and affirmers make great teammates. They're nice to have around, and we wish we had them to draw upon. But while it is good to ask if these people exist in our date books, it may be just as significant to question whether we fill these roles in the date books of others. For we not only need them on our team, but we need to be making it possible to serve on someone else's team.

A few sponsors and affirmers could have changed the climate in Bob Slocum's office. But they were nowhere to be found. The result? A tiring, boresome place where people lost their drive and desire to do their work well. A passionless place. You need a Mordecai in places like that.

16

More Special Friends

There are certain positions on a baseball team that almost no one wants to play. On the corner lot when the teams were chosen for the baseball game, it was clear that no one wanted to play catcher. "Joey, you catch," the captain would say, usually pointing to the little guy on the field.

"Oh come on," Joey would cry out, "I caught last week. Let Smitty do it. He can't catch fly balls anyway." The truth of the matter is that the catcher's job is dangerous. The catcher gets sore knees from crouching, bruises from thrown bats, and aches from collisions with sliding runners at home plate. Being the catcher simply isn't an enviable job.

The team of special friends also has a position that is unpleasant. I call it the position of the rebuker.

3. The Rebuker

It takes courage to include the *rebuker* on the team. For what he or she says often hurts and leaves bruises on the spirit. *But we may be talking about the most important member among our special friends.* We all need truth-tellers, even if we don't really want them. Pass them up or avoid them, and spiritual passion may be in great jeopardy.

The writers of the book of Proverbs put a great premium on the position of the rebuker: "Open rebuke is better than hidden love! Wounds from a friend are better than kisses from an enemy" (Prov. 27:5,6 TLB).

Truth-telling is in short supply in our world. Our relationships often include those who are willing to speak the truth behind our backs but not in front. The former is destructive; the latter constructive. Conversely, many of us who have been given the responsibility of leadership actually fear the truth because we get used to the feeling of being right, of being the person with the right answers. So it bothers us when someone comes along to tell us that we don't have everything together after all. Thus, the issue of truth-telling is a two-sided problem. Not many people want to *tell* the truth when it's painful, and not a lot of people want to *hear* the truth if it's painful.

Back to Joseph Heller's novel *Something Happened*. Bob Slocum describes a work world where people aren't truthful with one another either.

> People in the company are almost never fired; if they grow inadequate or obsolete ahead of schedule, they are encouraged to retire early or are eased aside into hollow, insignificant, newly created positions with fake functions and no authority, where they are sheepish and unhappy for as long as they remain; nearly always, they must occupy a small and less convenient office, sometimes with another person already in it; or, if they are still young, they are simply encouraged directly (though with courtesy) to find better jobs with other companies and then resign. Even the wide-awake young branch manager with the brilliant

185

future who got drunk and sick one afternoon and threw up into the hotel swimming pool during the company convention in Florida two years ago wasn't fired, although everyone knew he would not be permitted to remain. He knew it, too. Probably nothing was ever said to him. But he knew it. And four weeks after the convention ended, he found a better job with another company and resigned (Heller, *Something Happened*, p. 37).

No one wins in such a world. At first it is thought that people are simply protecting each other, watching out for each other's feelings. But no one grows where truth is absent. No one is pushed *to be* and *to do* the best. And when you look at this deficit from a Christian perspective, it describes a situation where men and women are never going to become all that God has made them to be nor will they gather the spiritual energy or passion to make it happen.

Recently I faced a traumatic week. I had appointments with three people or groups who examined aspects of my life with intense care—my doctor, who gave me my annual physical; my tax man, who carefully studied my financial picture; and the appraisal and review task force of InterVarsity's Board of Trustees, who wanted to investigate my year's performance as president.

Their jobs? To uncover any places where I have been abusing or misusing my body, my assets, or my job. To point out places where I can do better, avoid problems, and perform with greater excellence. You could call them the potential rebukers in my larger circle of special friends. In all three cases, I would have been silly to have avoided the encounters or to have refused to listen to what they had to say to me.

And yet some people do. I have acquaintances who will always avoid a physical, who apparently cut corners in their financial dealings, and who refuse to listen to experienced counselors critique their way of doing their work or developing their spiritual lives.

One rarely grows without a rebuke. One solid and loving rebuke is worth a hundred affirmations. Rebukes are the purifiers which keep spiritual passion clear and forceful.

A significant portion of Paul's letters to Timothy are actually rebuke. Paul was disturbed that the young man he'd been sponsoring was losing his passion to pastorally confront people. There were older men in the church who were spiritually lazy and there were those who were spreading inaccurate teaching. Timothy may have been pulling his punches. But Paul wasn't going to pull his. Preach! Exhort! Don't permit people to back you down. So went Paul's rebukes and admonitions. Presumably, Timothy was galvanized into action when he received the strong words of his sponsor/rebuker.

The rebukes of Jesus to Peter must have been stinging. "You're looking at this from a human point of view and not from God's" (Mark 8:33 TLB), he says at one time. "You will deny me three times" (Mark 14:30 RSV), he said some time later when Peter was long on words and generally short on performance. "Asleep? Couldn't you watch with me even one hour?" (Mark 14:37 TLB), he asked in the garden.

When Peter did indeed deny the Lord in the high priest's court, "the Lord turned and looked at Peter" (Luke 22:61 RSV). In this case a look was as good as a word. Later on the Galilee shoreline around a breakfast fire, Peter again heard the rebuke of Jesus. "What is that to you?" Jesus said when the impulsive disciple began to ask questions about another teammate while Jesus wanted him thinking about his own call (see John 21:22). In effect the Savior was saying, "Mind your own business and follow me."

187

Rebuke and criticism are two different things, the former a valued gift, the latter somewhat cheaper. But I have been taught even to seize the truth in a criticism that may have been leveled for reasons other than for building me up. "There is a kernel of truth in every criticism," I am told Dawson Trotman used to say to his friends. "Look for it, and when you find it, rejoice in its value."

I find that some younger men and women around me bristle at the hint of any rebuke or criticism. Their self-image is suddenly on the line, and you can feel their instinct rising to fight back like that of a cornered animal. But a great mark has been reached when we accept what seems to be a negative word and absorb it, forcing ourselves to grow in the reception, both examining the truth we hear and choosing not to fight back and hurt the one who played the rebuking position.

Looking back, I realize that rebukes were and still are among my greatest learning moments. They set me free from things that otherwise would have destroyed my spiritual passion. They spotlighted things that were hurting me badly but that I did not understand. So I am thankful to my wife and other special friends who play the position of rebuker on my team of special friends. I understand the proverb that says, "In the end, people appreciate frankness more than flattery" (Prov. 28:23 TLB).

I have often told the story of my special friend, Philip Armstrong, a missionary leader lost in a plane crash in Alaska. We were walking along a Japanese street when I made a derogatory comment about a mutual acquaintance. "Gordon," Armstrong immediately said, "a man of God would not say such a thing about another person." I was exposed and knew it. He was right. The rebuke stung, and I lived with its pain for many days afterward. But I will always be thankful for that rebuke, painful as it was, because I hear those words every time I am about to embarrass myself with a needless comment about another person. That was a rebuke that forced me to grow.

If you enjoy being a rebuker, think again about whether or not you are a special friend. Paul tells the Corinthians that he rebukes them with tears. Christ rebukes at the expense of His life. Jeremiah admits that he is so exhausted from rebuking that he wants to run into the desert and forget the whole thing.

The rebuker plays his or her position at great risk. And we, who at any moment become the rebuked, must be careful to listen intently, thanking the rebuker for truth that was shared at such high cost.

Elsewhere I have spoken of my favorite character in English church history, Charles Simeon. Simeon often struggled with irritability and impatience. It showed one night when he visited at the home of a friend, Mr. Edwards. Edwards later wrote to William Carus, Simeon's first biographer, about an encounter between Simeon and a servant:

> We were sitting at dinner when a servant behind [Simeon] stirred the fire, in a way so *unscientific*, that Mr. S. turned round and hit the man a thump on the back, to stay his proceedings. When he was leaving me, on horseback, after the same visit, my servant had put the wrong bridle upon his horse. He was in a hurry to be gone, and his temper broke out so violently, that I ventured to give him a little humorous castigation.

Then Mr. Edwards became a bit creative in his rebuke as he continues to describe.

> His cloak bag was to follow him by coach; so I feigned a

letter in my servant's name, saying, how high his character stood in the kitchen; but that they could not understand, how a gentleman, who preached and prayed so well, should be in such passions about nothing, and wear no *bridle* upon his own tongue. This I signed "John Softly", and deposited it in his cloak bag. The hoax so far succeeded, that at first he scarcely discovered it. . . .

But Charles Simeon was not dumb. He soon realized that the letter from "John Softly" was actually from his special friend, Mr. Edwards, and playing out the charade he penned a return letter addressed to Mr. "John Softly."

I most cordially thank you, my dear friend, for your kind and seasonable reproof. I feel it to be both just and necessary: and will endeavor with God's help to make a suitable improvement of it. If it do not produce its proper effects, I shall be exceedingly thankful to have a second edition of it. I trust your "precious balm will not break my head;" but I hope it will soften the spirit of your much indebted friend.

[signed] Charles. Proud and Irritable

Later Simeon wrote directly to Mr. Edwards about the incident and said

I have day and night thanked God for you, and prayed for blessings on your head, and watched and prayed against my besetting sins. . . . I hope, my dearest brother, that when you find your soul nigh to God, you will remember one who so greatly needs all the help he can get . . . (Carus, *Memories of the Life of Rev. Charles Simeon,* p. 112).

But let us go on to other players on the team of special

friends who renew and help to maintain our spiritual passion.

4. The Intercessor

If I am to gain spiritual passion from my special friends, among them will be those who play the position of the *intercessor*. Intercessors are those who have accepted the responsibility for holding me up to God in prayer.

Gail and I have enjoyed a number of intercessors in our lives. You can spot them. They carefully ask questions about the issues you're facing, the trips you will soon be taking, the problems you're trying to solve. And you know they have not been merely curious when they follow up a few weeks later to say, "I've been praying every day about ————; what's happening? What's God doing?"

One of the most fascinating (but also frightening) examples of intercession I ever heard about came from the mouth of a Salvation Army officer who was praying over some of the first officers of the Army to leave England for America in 1860. He prayed:

> Lord, these ladies are going to America to preach the gospel. If they are fully given up to Thee, be with them and bless them and grant them success. But if they are not faithful, drown'em, Lord; drown'em.

Jesus plays the role of intercessor when he sadly confronts Peter about his proneness to denial: "Simon, Simon, behold, Satan demanded to have you, that he might sift you like wheat, *but I have prayed for you* that your faith may not fail; and when you have turned again, strengthen your brethren" (Luke 22:31,32 RSV, emphasis added).

191

The entire seventeenth chapter of John is a model of intercessory prayer. "I am praying for them" (John 17:9 RSV), Christ says to the Father. That they might be kept from the evil one (v. 15). That they might be one (v. 21). That they would be where He is (v. 24). He prayed as a special friend. When Jesus ascended to Heaven, He assumed the position of intercessor for the Christian, and He plays that position in our lives even now.

"A Christian fellowship lives and exists by the intercession of its members for one another," writes Dietrich Bonhoeffer, "or it collapses."

> I can no longer condemn or hate a brother for whom I pray, no matter how much trouble he causes me. His face, hitherto may have been strange and intolerable to me, is transformed in intercession into the countenance of a brother for whom Christ died, the face of a forgiven sinner. This is a happy discovery for the Christian who begins to pray for others. There is no dislike, no personal tension, no estrangement that cannot be overcome by intercession as far as our side of it is concerned. Intercessory prayer is the purifying bath into which the individual and the fellowship must enter every day. The struggle we undergo with our brother in intercession may be a hard one, but that struggle has the promise that it will gain its goal. . . . To make intercession means to grant our brother the same right that we have received, namely to stand before Christ and share his mercy (Bonhoeffer, *Life Together*, quoted in Benson and Benson, *Disciplines of the Inner Life*, p. 71).

E. Stanley Jones, the great evangelist, once wrote of a time early in his Christian experience. "For months after my conversion," he wrote, "I was running under cloudless skies. And then suddenly I tripped, almost fell, pulled back this side of the sin, but was shaken and humiliated that I could come that close to sin. I thought I was emancipated and found I wasn't."

Then he goes on to write of the effort of special friends who played the intercessory position:

> I went to the class meeting—I'm grateful that I didn't stay away—went, but my (spiritual) music had gone. I had hung my harp on a weeping willow tree. As the others spoke of their joys and victories of the week, I sat there with the tears rolling down my cheeks. I was heartbroken. After the others had spoken, John Zink, the class leader, said: "Now, Stanley, tell us what is the matter." I told them I couldn't but would they please pray for me? Like one man they fell to their knees, and they lifted me back to the bosom of God by faith and love. When we got up from our knees, I was reconciled. The universe opened its arms and took me in again. The estrangement was gone. I took my heart from the willow tree and began to sing again. . . . (Jones, *A Song of Ascents*, p. 42).

Who are our intercessors? Anyone in Christian leadership should set a goal for himself to identify and regularly connect with at least three intercessors who will "play" on his or her ministry "team." These intercessors should be capable of generating a constant flow of praise or concern as they pray. Their prayers will provide a protective curtain about the one who is engaged in spiritual warfare. And a major part of the intercessors' prayers would be that our spiritual passion be constantly renewed and that we not grow weary.

193

5. The Partner

Another player on our team of special friends is the generalist, the roving fielder if you please. That player is the *partner*. The restoration and maintenance of spiritual passion frequently depends upon the process of partnership with one or more who share the load. In fact, I am not sure that most of us can ever reach the full extent of our energies if we are not in partnership with someone else.

Unfortunately, we are in a day when there are not many outstanding examples of partnership, but such partnerships are beautiful to behold. The partnership of the Billy Graham team for more than forty years has been an inspiration to all who have watched from a distance. This group of men heard a call from God early in their adulthood, and they banded together for Billy Graham to pursue the goal of world evangelization. And while the world has celebrated the amazing success of Billy Graham, it has not recognized that, humanly speaking, a share of the credit goes to the men about him who quietly gave him courage, insight, and strength. They chose to martial their energies and pour them into him much like the jump start that is necessary for a weak car battery.

I often wonder how many men and women there are whom God could probably have used more effectively had they been a part of a team that included partners. It is not unusual to hear of gifted men and women who fell short of goals they should have met. What happened? Perhaps they—or those about them—refused to act like partners, choosing rather to pursue their own private goals and aims.

A close friend told me that one draft horse can move two tons of weight. But two draft horses in harness, working together, can move twenty-three tons of weight. That prob-

194

ably is not far from properly illustrating how men and women can work together in a common objective.

For many of us, a spouse is the first-line partner. My wife, Gail, has been a partner in Christian growth and service since the day we married. On many occasions, this has meant that one of us (usually Gail) forsook some privilege or personal desire in order to stand alongside the other and provide the support needed to respond to God's call and direction.

Partners pick up a part of the load and accept responsibility for it. Nothing is too menial or too outrageous if partners believe in one another.

One of the great marital partnerships in Christian service was that of Hudson and Maria Taylor. J. C. Pollock, describing the strength that moved between the Taylors, wrote:

> Hudson would lean hard on her, drawing vigor from her spiritual maturity, her tranquility and faith, her unwaivering affection. She gave him and their work all she had, every ounce of strength, every thought that crossed her intelligent mind, all the force of her love. She allowed him to drain her, and if sometimes his demands were unconsciously selfish, she was no more aware of it than he (Pollock, *Hudson Taylor and Maria,* p. 172).

Dixon Hoste, deeply impressed by the Taylors, was one of the famed Cambridge Seven, a group of young university men who shocked all of England in the late 1800s when they decided to abandon great careers to go overseas as missionaries.

One of the young missionaries, Stanley Smith, invited Hoste to work with him but insisted that he, Smith, would have to be the leader since he had a little more qualification in terms of experience than Hoste.

Hoste, ever the competitor, found this invitation to partnership where he would be the second man a bit hard to take.

> I was ruffled in my spirit. Why should I serve under him? We were about the same age, and had come to China together. Granted he was brilliant with the language, could make easy contacts, and in other ways was my superior, this did not seem sufficient reason to me, so I suggested he should write to the Mission at Shanghai for a younger man, as it was their business to make appointments.

But Hoste was a godly man who was open even to inner rebuke, and he remained thoughtful.

> Later on thinking over the situation, the Spirit of God probed me, and I was forced to admit that I did not relish the thought of being under my friend. I thought of my "face," what friends would surmise, etc. The difficulty was in my own heart. It was impressed upon me that the unwillingness persisted in would mean my having to part company with the Lord Jesus Christ, who dwells with the humble ones, those who willingly go down. I therefore accepted my friend's suggestion, and we worked happily together for several months . . . (Hoste, *If I Am to Lead,* p. 53).

There are of course the great partnerships in the Scriptures which give us a model of this relationship that maintains or renews spiritual passion. The partnership of Paul and Barnabas is probably the most beautiful of all.

It began with Barnabas's desire to sponsor Paul at

Jerusalem when he needed an introduction into the church. It became a partnership when Barnabas later went to Tarsus, Paul's hometown, to find him and invite him to Antioch where a team ministry was needed. The partnership hit its full stride as the men began to travel the world engaging in evangelism and planting churches.

Paul was wise enough to realize that he could never operate well without partners. At almost every point in his ministry he linked up with others called "fellow-soldiers," "brothers," or "yokefellows." When he wrote to Timothy (2 Timothy 4:9ff) he shared information on the movements of all his partners: those whom he had sent out, those who had deserted him, those who were still there. And it is very clear that Paul did not like to be without partners in his life and work.

In Robert Sherwood's remarkable account of the partnership between Harry Hopkins and President Franklin D. Roosevelt, a conversation between FDR and Wendell Willkie, who had just been defeated by Roosevelt in the 1941 election, is described. Willkie was about to head for wartorn London, and he had been invited to the White House for a brief visit with the president before he embarked. Roosevelt told him that he would appreciate it if Willkie would visit with Harry Hopkins, whom Willkie would find in London on another assignment.

Wendell Willkie's immediate reaction was negative since he and many other Americans disliked Hopkins intensely. At that point, Sherwood writes, Willkie asked FDR a "pointed question:"

Why do you keep Hopkins so close to you? You surely must realize that people distrust him and they resent his influence.

197

Willkie quoted Roosevelt as replying: "I can understand that you wonder why I need that half-man around me." (The "half-man" was an allusion to Hopkins' extreme physical frailty.) "But—someday you may well be sitting here where I am now as President of the United States. And when you are, you'll be looking at that door over there and knowing that practically everybody who walks through it wants something out of you. You'll learn what a lonely job this is, and you'll discover the need for somebody like Harry Hopkins who asks for nothing except to serve you" (Sherwood, *Roosevelt and Hopkins*, p. 2).

6. The Pastor

There is one more player on the team of special friends—the *pastor*. This is the tender person, the person who comes alongside in the moment of exhaustion. The pastor—and I'm not necessarily talking about ordained ministers—is the one who helps make sense out of life when all has become confusing.

Dr. C. Henry Kempe, a specialist in pediatrics and microbiology, once wrote of his experiences in an intensive care unit in Bellevue Hospital in New York when he was recovering from a heart attack. It was an extremely difficult period marked with pain and mental confusion. "I have no memory whatever of the first two weeks of my stay, but the subsequent weeks are very clear in my mind. On recollection what stands out is the exquisite nursing care I received." He goes on:

I remember that when I first emerged from a haze of pain and confusing procedures, each nurse coming on shift in this large twelve-bed unit would introduce herself by her first name, tell me what day and time it was, and, almost

198

without fail, hold one of my hands in her two hands while looking straight into my eyes. I found this very comforting, because I was aware of having lost not only considerable intellectual ability, but I also was having frightening hallucinatory experiences. *These were immediately wiped out by this personal contact.* The nurses would explain what they called "scary dreams" and thus reassure me about the frequency of hallucinations. They said that everybody who has lost a lot of REM sleep was likely to hallucinate; that it was a routine experience in their patients; that these images invariably went away, and that I was neither stupid nor going crazy. During those days the repeated reassurance about regaining intelligence and sanity was perhaps the most important event of the daily nursing contact (Kempe, *Pharos*).

In a medical metaphor, Kempe has described what a pastor does on our team to help restore and maintain our spiritual passion. The word pastor means shepherd; it describes the function of one who leads, feeds, and protects.

Spiritual passion or energy is usually dissipated in the midst of fear and confusion. That is why we need to have in our circle of special friends the one who senses our restiveness and speaks to it in words and gestures.

While I have been a pastor to many, I have also known the need for a pastor. I can recall a short period of serious personal turbulence in which a pastor came alongside with the tender question, "Are there knots in your life today, Gordon?" And he opened the door to a conversation that led to my gaining a more even perspective on what God might be saying. And then my friend concluded the conversation by laying his hands upon me and praying for my strength and guidance.

Gail and I will always recall the visit of another pastor

199

friend when we thought our young daughter was dying. He brought calmness to the hospital waiting room as he sat with us, not always talking, but always there to be our strength and to understand the nature of our panic.

Our special-friend team needs such a person to whom we can turn in a moment of danger. But when I look about at those in Christian leadership and I ask, "Who is your pastor?" I am impressed with the large number whose answer is, "I really have no pastor, no one to whom I would feel comfortable to turn to."

The apostle Paul was a special-friend pastor to a terrified group of soldiers and sailors in the midst of a Mediterranean storm when he intervened in the midst of their panic:

> I now bid you take heart; for there will be no loss of life among you, but only of the ship. For this very night there stood by me an angel of the God to whom I belong and whom I worship, and he said "Do not be afraid, Paul. . . ." So take heart, men, for I have faith in God that it will be exactly as I have been told (Acts 27:22–25 RSV).

This description of performance by sponsors, affirmers, rebukers, intercessors, partners, and pastors is a long way from the sort of people Bob Slocum talked about in Joseph Heller's novel *Something Happened*. His world was one of extreme exhaustion. But the world of the person with special friends is filled with energy and power. The spiritual passion of that person will be renewed to overflowing.

17

Renewing Your Spiritual Passion

In a wonderful book, *The Table of Inwardness*, Calvin Miller wrote of an antique wooden dynamite box in his home. The box was made in the nineteenth century, Miller said, carefully constructed to withstand shock as its explosive contents were transported from the manufacturer to a place of use.

On the lid were large red and black letters which said DANGER DYNAMITE! "But the last I saw it," Miller wrote, "it was filled with common paraphernalia that could be found in any workroom."

I'm drawn to the irony of Calvin Miller's description of a box designed for dynamite which warns that it contains dynamite but which now stores only "common paraphernalia."

This might be the unfortunate picture of the wearied follower of God who has lost heart, whose spiritual passion is nonexistent. Like the box, a man or woman is created to store spiritual dynamite, the marvelous energy of God. And (here the analogy begins to break down) he or she is created to discharge that dynamite. Furthermore, this person is often thrust into situations where the capacity of that heavenly dynamite is verbally affirmed and historically recounted.

We're talking about a person who gets highly involved in a church or religious organization, who attempts to live congenially in the marketplace and in the neighborhood, who would really like to be noted as *trying* to be a pleasure to God. But something is amiss. Either the dynamite is wet or *it really isn't even there*. It's as good as having common paraphernalia within.

When I set out to write this book, I had a difficult time trying to explain to interested people what I was writing about. "Weariness," I would say in response to their questions concerning the topic. "Well, what do you mean by that?" they would ask.

"I'm concerned about the fact that people are doing more, knowing more, and trying to take on more, but in many cases not really getting any further any faster. The worst case under these circumstances is the specter of some folks who just end up dropping out. They get spiritually tired trying to do and say the right things. But they feel a quiet frustration, and they feel as if they're going nowhere. Somehow we've not helped them; we've only given them more guilt or more things to do. So they're gone!"

"Oh you're talking about stress and burnout," comes back the rejoinder. "We need to hear more about that."

"But I'm not sure I'm talking about stress and burnout," I try to say. "I'm talking about something that's deeper than that, a spiritual sensation that can hardly be described apart from the word 'weary.'" What started as a pilgrimage has degenerated into a rat race. And the rats are winning.

"And the King . . . arrived weary at the Jordan; and there he refreshed himself" went the phrase we contemplated in earlier chapters. What did David feel like when he knew that he'd tried his best, given his all, worked his hardest? What was the spiritual fatigue he sensed as he

202

sat there on the edge of the river washing the grime of hurried travel off of his body? Where could he go from there? What could he do?

That Davidic sensation may be old, but it is not obsolete. I strongly suspect that literally millions of evangelical Christians in this world have dropped out of the visible activities of the family of God because they're tired or weary.

Talk to them and find out how they feel. It is not bitterness about which they speak, not even disillusionment. They simply shrug their shoulders and say, "It didn't work for me. I haven't abandoned Jesus, but I'm tired of all the activity that people say has to be done in the name of Jesus."

To seize a piece of Calvin Miller's analogy, these people decided one day that having DANGER DYNAMITE written on the surface performance but having little more than religious paraphernalia within was an inadequate way to live. It is a hypocrisy of sorts; a gap in integrity. "I don't like singing songs that quote me as saying or doing something when I know in my heart that I'm not there and—at this rate—never will be," a spiritually discouraged man once told me.

I would like to propose that what these people needed— and didn't find or didn't take the time for—were things like safe places, still times, and special friends. The safe places would have allowed them to find out *who* God is. The still times would have given them a chance to *hear* what God says. The special friends would have made possible the encouragement and correctives for them to *obey* what God *asks*.

But all too often our safe places are too noisy. Our still times are clogged with busyness. And our special friends are little more than acquaintances who don't know or care how to deal with us in this category of life (nor we for them). The result? Weariness, which is to say, loss of spiritual passion, loss of the energy to get on with and produce what Christ called an abundant life.

The secret to spiritual passion, someone may say, is the great enthusiasm spawned in the large and frequent meetings and conferences that Christians can put on better than anyone else. Pack it full with soloists, special speakers, and a thousand seminars. Let us get excited by the numbers of people, the humor and scintilating observations of the teachers, and the new approaches to faith that sharp minds can manufacture.

"No, that's not it," another may argue. "The secret to spiritual passion is the Holy Spirit. I'm surprised you didn't mention that a lot earlier in this book. Just relax and let Him do whatever He wants to do through you. It's worked for me, and I'm positive it will work for you."

"Forget all of that. You've missed it," a third may suggest. "Spiritual passion comes from being exposed to the real world and by seeing the needs of people. Get overseas; go to the ghetto; visit in a mental hospital. You'll get passion quickly!"

Perhaps there is something useful in all of those interpretive answers. Each rests on passages of Scripture that seem to strongly undergird the proffered argument. But the fact is that many Christians, pursuing each line of reasoning, still fall short of the promised results. And no rational explanation seems to help us understand why.

Perhaps we do not adequately visualize what we're searching for when we talk about spiritual passion. We're not positive what actually pleases the God of the Bible when we seek intimacy with Him. And beyond that, we're not entirely confident that we know how He wishes us to act as His children in this broken world.

Is it too dumb a question to ask all over again what might a spiritually passionate person look like? Not all of us can be well-known heroes, speakers, authors, liberators, or organizational heads. Is that what a spiritually passionate person looks like? One might have reason to think so because those roles tend to be the models we hoist up before one another as worthy of emulation.

But there are so many millions of us common, ordinary people, men and women whose lives are routine—making a home for a family, coping as a single, trying to get or keep a job, nursing along a troubled automobile we can't afford to replace, being concerned about retirement, wondering whether or not we're going to amount to anything. What does the spiritually passionate life look like in these contexts?

A somewhat obscure story in the Older Testament might provide a valuable insight. The story appears in 1 Chronicles 11 and recalls a period of time in David's life when, as usual, he found himself in hostile conditions, forced to flee to the desert or wilderness lifestyle to survive.

The enemy this time was the Philistines, a hostile tribe on the southern border of Israel. The Philistines were strong, and their armies were momentarily victorious against David's people. At the time of the story, they held strong positions around Bethlehem, David's original hometown.

Certain men of Israel had drifted into the hills to join David, and from the ranks of what we might call today a guerrilla army came a cadre of what I would like to call special friends, mighty men known for their loyalty and bravery. The word used to describe them was the Hebrew word *hesed* meaning, among other things, "devoted."

You can assume that David was tired of running, tired of living in caves, probably tired in general of being at war. In a quiet moment, David spoke out with some nostalgia. "Oh that some one would give me water to drink from the well of Bethlehem" (1 Chron. 11:17 RSV).

It was clearly not a command that David gave; not even a call for volunteers. *Merely a wish!* And it is important to remember that because of what subsequently happened. Just a wish from the lips of David, but enough of a wish that three of David's mighty men heard it and immediately determined to deliver water as a gift from the Bethlehem well as soon as possible (see 1 Chron. 11:18).

Children have thrilled to the story of the three unnamed men who set out to fight their way through the Philistine lines, draw the brand name water David had been thinking about and, fighting their way back the same way they came, present it to him as an act of intense affection.

So moved was David by this action that he could not drink the water but wisely poured it out on the ground as a drink offering to God. He knew devotion when he saw it, and he appreciated the fact that no human being was worthy of the intense devotion these three men had given to him. The water had to be redesignated as a gift to David's God. A good decision.

I am indebted to my friend Dr. Edwin Clowney for pointing out this passage in an InterVarsity seminar where I was a cospeaker. I was deeply moved as I saw the picture of devotion he painted in his exposition of the passage. In a moment I knew that the three mighty men of David had established a pattern of performance that most describes the man or woman whose spiritual passion is clear and forceful.

THREE POWERFUL TRUTHS THAT PUT THE CHRISTIAN LIFE IN PERSPECTIVE

I saw in the actions of those mighty men a simple but powerful set of truths that put the Christian life in proper perspective. Their action symbolized the way a man or woman with spiritual passion lives.

Let me point out the truths that make this story so useful.

1. Intimacy Makes It Possible to Hear God's Wishes

The fact is that David's wish was most likely uttered quietly, informally. *You had to be in the presence of the commander to have heard it.*

Use your imagination and ask where the others were when this wish was made known. Doing good things, perhaps—pitching tents, shining boots, sharpening weapons, washing laundry, cooking food. All good and necessary activities. But the *best* activity for the moment seems to have been in the presence of the commander in chief, where not only commands could be heard, but also a few wishes.

To be in the presence of the Commander is to be in a *safe place*; and to hear his wishes demands a *still time* when listening is the most important thing. That's intimacy, and it generates passion, a desire to hear and to please. No hearing, no intimacy, no passion.

With my imagination still running, I can see those three mighty men sitting near the commander listening to every

207

word, anxious to know how they can, in fact, please. Theirs is a proactive listening: seeking the wishes of the one to whom they had devoted themselves.

They remind me of one of the unusual traits of my wife, Gail, who has a habit of listening carefully to the wishes of her husband and children. Unlike most of us, she has disciplined herself to write down what she hears. It is simply amazing how every Father's day or every birthday (or any other special day she can manufacture) includes little (or large) gifts that originated in the wistful comments of weeks before. The gifts tell me that she has listened carefully to the serendipitous musings of my heart.

Only in safe places and during still times will one hear the wishes of God—or of anyone else, for that matter. God's wishes are not shouted; often they are hidden behind the commands. Anyone can hear the commandments of God unless he chooses not to. But it takes a sensitive ear to hear the wishes of God, and that only comes—as I've said—in safe places at still times.

The intimacy of the commander's presence is something sought by relatively few people. In a world that offers too many experiences of easily achieved, and therefore cheapened, intimacy, not many people are willing to pay the price demanded to gain the presence of God.

"The incessant and sabbathless pursuit of a man's fortune leaveth out tribute which we owe to God of our time," Sir Francis Bacon wrote as he struggled with the balance in his life of ambition-oriented labor and the need to step back and ask what it all meant and where it was all going.

I have gained great assistance in the development of my own spiritual life as I have thought of the God who has wishes for His people and the world He has created. His commands are there for all to read and see; but His wishes are only for those who set out each day to listen eagerly and carefully.

I am amazed how often the wishes reveal themselves in the intimacy of time with Him: in the quiet moments and still times, in the tragic moments where there is pain and hopelessness, in the opportune moments when an act of potential servanthood presents itself.

When our date books and our personal road maps do not indicate the discipline of safe-place and still-time experiences, we forfeit the chance to monitor the wishes of God. We will have to depend upon what other people tell us, and their interpretations may not be accurate. Our neglect is a serious loss.

That is why I have learned that the time budgeted for safe-place/still-time activity is the most important single event in my daily lifestyle. Ignorance of this need leads to weariness.

2. The Choice to Act Is Often Taken at Great Risk

The accounts of this exciting story do not include any record of debate among the three men. "Are you crazy?" you can almost hear one of them say. "Do you know where that well is located, how strongly the area is fortified, how many people we'll have to mow down to get there? For water? For one man?"

Perhaps it is significant that the record does not indicate such a scenario. Probably because it didn't happen. The effort of the text is to indicate how devoted, passionate men really think and act. The wish of the general came through like a command to the devoted. The passion generated moved from a listening mode to an action mode.

Convictions generated from a genuine encounter with the living God *create* the passion to act and the strength to carry out the action. What all too often happens, I fear, is that modern Christians try to move on other people's passion: that of an organizational leader, a slick "sales" presentation made by a group that knows marketing and public relations techniques. We respond with genuine excitement, but it is a thin sort of passion easily dissipated or quickly supplanted by the next powerful message.

David's men heard the wish from the lips of their commander. The man or woman who takes the time to hear God speak is apt to have the same reaction: instant motion.

Moses heard the wishes of God at the burning bush. "I have heard the cries of my people. . . . I have seen their pain. . . . I have walked among them. . . . Moses, go and deliver them" (see Exod. 3:7–10). True, Moses was at first reluctant to respond to such a wish. He had lost his passion for heroic action the first time around when he'd killed an Egyptian. (He had probably intended then to be a liberating leader and then belatedly discovered that the Hebrew people weren't ready for heroes.)

But finally Moses responded, and with few exceptions he maintained a force of spiritual passion that carried a whole nation to the edge of the Promised Land (see Exod. 3, 4). But how did he keep it all going? By maintaining still times in safe places where he pursued the voice of God, the glory of God, the wishes of God. Busy as he was, he never lacked time to go to the mountain (see Exod. 19, 20).

John the Baptist also heard the wishes of God in the desert; Peter heard them on a rooftop; the apostle Paul on a lonely road. And the men acted. Mary, the mother of the Lord, heard the wishes of God in an appearance from an angel. She was surprised, to be sure, but she made a choice to act.

It is interesting to ponder the amount of action for which common people are responsible simply because of their willingness to listen and their choice to act, even at great risk.

In the biography of General William Booth, founder of the Salvation Army, a poignant moment is described when his son, Bramwell, must tell his father (then 83) that he is going blind from a disease of the eyes.

> "You mean that I am blind?"
>
> "Well, General, I fear that we must contemplate that."
> After a pause the old man said, "I shall never see your face again?"
>
> "No, probably not in this world."
> During the next few moments the veteran's hand crept along the counterpane to take hold of his son's, and holding it he said very calmly, "God must know best!" And after another pause, "Bramwell, I have done what I could for God and for the people with my eyes. Now I shall do what I can for God and for the people without my eyes" (Begbie, *The Life of General Wm Booth,* p. 422).

3. A Divine Energy Creates the Ultimate Passion

Throughout the Bible, a mysterious energy of God pulsates, which, when planted within people, makes for formidable accomplishment. We know that energy to be originated by the Holy Spirit, the third person of the Godhead.

In the earliest days of biblical history, that energy seemed to come to certain people for special opportunities. And

211

when it came, their passion grew and their performance was extraordinary. Joseph wisely serving as consultant to Egypt's pharaoh (see Gen. 41); David shutting out Goliath (see 1 Sam. 17:50); Gideon leading the charge against overwhelming odds (see Judg. 7, 8); Jeremiah confronting an unusually wicked king (see Jer. 37); Elizabeth providing support for the pregnant Mary (see Luke 1:42–45).

But the hope and expectation of people who sought God was that the passion and energy needed would be available for all people and that it would remain with them during the routine times as well as the unusual times.

I have always been convinced that this passion they sought was the normal life experience of the first man and woman who lived under optimum creation conditions before the fall of humanity. Theirs was the model life of spiritual passion. A daily intimacy with the Creator, the work of discovering the glories of the things created, the ecstasy of the resulting experience. This was a cycle of passion that captured the entire human experience: listening, working, enjoying.

Almost all of that was lost in the acts of disobedience when the first man and woman made a strange and awful choice to deviate from the commands and wishes of their God. Passion lost!

The Christian story is that of restoration. Restoration of intimacy with God and of the passion which comes from renewing our choice to respond to His wishes.

In our somewhat blinded condition, we as human beings have not always been intentional toward the things God wants to give His people. For example, in spite of the fact that Jesus promised His disciples this unusual passion or power, they seem to have remained ignorant as to what it all meant. Almost like a mother who must occasionally press

212

good things upon her children for their good, it would appear that God had to press passion into the apostles. But once they had their passion renewed, they charged into the streets of Jerusalem and began to act in a spirit of bravery and boldness that no one could ever have imagined. Little men become giants!

Down through the centuries, common and somewhat unskilled people have caused remarkable things to happen in their worlds when the passion of God invaded their beings. They took risks, overcame obstacles, and set standards that leave us breathless.

This is the effort of the Spirit of God as He comes to the wearied person. To enliven us, to envision us, to enpower us. And when He does, this is not to say that the primary objective is to make us feel good, or secure, or more successful as is sometimes implied in certain circles. Although some of those things may actually happen, the chief purpose is to enlarge our capacity to join the task of kingdom building: demonstrating in life and in word the splendor of the living Christ and His incredible power to rescue lost people and turn them around to a higher life. "You shall receive power," Christ said, "and you shall be my witnesses" (Acts 1:8 RSV).

I have taken a lot of pages to say a simple thing, something I'm afraid has often gotten buried beneath a host of religious procedures and processes. We have over-complicated our God and His ways of coming to us. We have organized Him, strategized Him, and compartmentalized Him. We have reduced His ways of working with us to cute little formulas, and we have stood off in our own corners critical of others who seek His face in ways that differ from our own temperaments or styles of perception. But it is clear that God longs to renew a spiritual passion within us.

Few rules lead to this renewal, and they appear to be disarmingly simple. I for one am tired of those who have claimed otherwise.

For the man or woman at the edge of a Jordan, wearied by too many choices and burdened with too many obligations, there is a simple formula: safe places, still times, and special friends.

The combination provides enough room for the faithful God of Jesus Christ to begin to speak to us. Drawn near under such circumstances, we begin to hear Him speak. At first it is a struggle to silence the interfering noises, but God has never made it a problem to approach Him. He does not play games with us, hiding first here and then there until we figure Him out. He is rather straightforward about all of this. *He wants to be heard.* Why have we made it so tough on ourselves?

I have met many passionate people. They come in all ages, from all backgrounds, with all sorts of personal capacities. No two look alike. But you know them when you see them. They are not hurried; they are not shrill; they are not out to impress.

You know them because when you come into their presence; they make you think of Christ. Somehow you feel that you have just understood a little more of what it was like to be in the presence of Jesus.

The energy that pushes them along is not the thunderous noise of a jet, nor the pressure of a Niagara. It's a quiet energy that you sense even if you can't see it.

I suppose what I'm talking about is best seen up at Peace Ledge, our New Hampshire retreat. An enormous rock is in the woods. Rather, *two* rocks. There used to be one, but it is split in two. And it is clear why there is a split.

214

Long ago (who knows how long?) water seeped into a crevice, froze, and created a deeper split. Then a seed blew into the deepened crack and germinated. From that tiny seed a tree began to grow, and its inexorable development simply pushed the rock apart. Now there are two rocks and a tree right in the middle. That's a quiet passion, quiet, indefatigable, powerful.

That kind of passion quietly splits apart the hardness of hate, greed, and intemperance. It lodges in the crevices of the home, the church, and society. It breaks up things and starts something new. That is the kind of passion we need in this passionless world of ours. And it comes from people who have decided to take the time and to go to the places and establish themselves among the people who can help us hear God speak.

I began this book with a reflection on a childhood memory, a dark Canadian road that my family traveled so long ago. Thinking of those moments, I again remember how tired and frustrated we were: having traveled too far to turn back and yet not knowing whether we had enough fuel or energy to keep moving ahead.

As I replay that night's journey in my mind, I suddenly see a light on the horizon. We drive on, the light getting brighter. And then we are there. The light illuminates a sign: WEARY TRAVELERS WELCOME, VACANCY.

Soon our family is in a small cabin. Our irritabilities are quickly dispelled; we lie down to rest, and soon we are asleep. The weariness of that day that had deflated our enthusiasm for a vacation trip drains away in the nighttime hours. The next morning parents and children will rise again, the prospects and the passion for a continued journey brighter than ever. The night is forgotten.

215

Holy Father,

In the frenzy of our modern lives at home, in the market place, and in the church, keep before us your invitation to intimacy.

Help us to locate those safe places, where in still times you will speak into our spirits from your Word, by your Spirit, through our special friends. May we learn as a result how to live in pursuit of your wishes.

For all who are weary, empty of spirit, directionless or numb, I pray for the renewal of spiritual passion. The reason? To be a pleasure to you and a light to the world.

AMEN.

SOURCES

Begbie, Harold. *The Life of General Wm Booth*. New York: Mac-Millan, 1920.

Benson, Bob, and Michael Benson. *Disciplines of the Inner Life*. Waco, Tex.: Word Books, 1985.

Bonhoeffer, Dietrich. *Life Together*. New York: Harper & Row, 1976.

Bowen, Catherine Drinker. *Francis Bacon: The Temper of a Man*. Boston: Little Brown and Co., 1963.

Bruce, A. B. *The Training of the Twelve*. Grand Rapids: Kregel Publishers, 1979.

Carus, William. *Memories of the Life of Rev. Charles Simeon*. American Edition. New York: Robert Cartier, 1848.

Cowman, Lettie. *Springs in the Valley*. Grand Rapids: Zondervan, 1939.

Eisenhower, D. D. *At Ease: Stories I Tell My Friends*. New York: Doubleday, 1967, quoted in *Harvard Business Review*.

Fénelon, François. *Spiritual Letters to Women*. Grand Rapids: Zondervan, 1984.

Gilkey, Langdon. *Shantung Compound*. New York: Harper & Row, 1966.

Guinness, Howard. *Journey Among Students*. Sydney, Australia: Anglican Information Office, 1978.

Hefley, James, and Marti Hefley. *By Their Blood: Christian Martyrs of the 20th Century*. Milford, Mich.: Mott Media, 1979.

Heller, J. *Something Happened*. New York: Ballantine Books, 1979.

Hoste, D. E. *If I Am to Lead*. Robesonia, Penn.: OMF Books, 1968.

Jensen, Margaret. *Lena*. San Bernardino, Calif.: Heres Life, 1985.

Jones, E. Stanley. *A Song of Ascents: A Spiritual Autobiography*. Nashville: Abingdon Press, 1979.

Kempe, C. Henry. *Pharos*. Winter 1979.

Kramer, Jerry, ed. *Lombardi: Winning Is the Only Thing*. New York: Pocket Books, 1970.

Laubach, Frank. *Frank Laubach: Letters by a Modern Mystic*. Syracuse, N.Y.: New Readers Press, 1979.

Lean, Garth. *God's Politician*. London: Darton, Longman & Todd, 1980.

Lenski, R. C. H. *The Interpretation of St. Paul's First and Second Epistles to the Corinthians*. Minneapolis: Augsburg Publishing House, 1937.

Miller, Calvin. *The Table of Inwardness*. Downers Grove, Ill.: InterVarsity Press, 1984.

Nouwen, Henri. *Clowning in Rome*. New York: Doubleday and Co., 1979.

Nouwen, Henri. *Reaching Out*. New York: Doubleday, 1975.

Palmer, Earl. *Alive from the Center*. Waco, Tex.: Word Books, 1982.

Pearson, Hesketh. *Oscar Wilde: His Life and Wit*. New York: Harper & Brothers, 1946.

Pennington, M. Basil. *Centering Prayer: Renewing an Ancient Christian Prayer Form*. New York: Image Books, 1982.

Phillips, J. B. *Your God Is Too Small*. New York: MacMillan, 1961.

Pollock, J. C. *Hudson Taylor and Maria*. New York: McGraw Hill, 1962.

Quoist, Michael. *With Open Heart*. New York: Crossroads, 1983.

Sangster, Paul. *Doctor Sangster*. London: Epworth Press, 1962.

Sherwood, Robert. *Roosevelt and Hopkins*. New York: Universal Library, rev. 1950.

Sproul, R. C. *Stronger Than Steel: The Wayne Alderson Story*. San Francisco: Harper & Row, 1980.

Turnbull, Ralph G. *A Minister's Obstacles*. Westwood, N.J.: Fleming H. Revell Co., 1964.

STUDY GUIDE

Preface: The Dark-Road Times

P.1   Why are you reading this book?

P.2   Recall a recent time of "mindless" or "spiritless" journey (p. 6).

P.3   Read the account of Simon Peter in John 21:3–13. How do you know that his spiritual passion was renewed (p. 7)?

P.4   Based on the analogy of the unmarked "road of life" (p. 7), where are you now?

P.5   Reflect on your conversation in the last six months (inner or spoken). Is there any work which you have repeated with great longing?

P.6   On a scale of 1–10, where would you rate your passion to be godly (p. 8)?

P.7   Identify your formula for being transported above the "ordinary and ineffective" (p. 8). It is a helpful formula?

P.8   Draw a time line of your Christian life (or spiritual journey, if you are not a follower of Christ). Mark some high or peak times and some rough times (p. 9).

P.9   The author raises some questions in the final paragraph of page 10. What is potentially tiring or draining for you? How were these issues faced by former travelers? Would their advice help you?

1: It's Got to Glow in You All the Time

1.1   What do you think of the author's use of the word *passion* in the context of athletic domination (pp. 11–12) or academic research (pp. 13–14)?

1.2   Identify several of the most passionate moments in your life.

1.3   Add to your list any passions that "provide fuel" for leaders in addition to power, notoriety, and raw achievement (p. 14).

1.4   What do you usually say about the passionate people in the main areas of your life, such as home, work, or church? Compare your answer with the paragraph at the bottom of page 15.

1.5   Memorize Paul's statement of passion in Philippians 3:13–14 (p. 16).

1.6   Find the author's sentence that summarizes his purpose for this book (p. 17). Rewrite it in your own words.

1.7 How does the mature Christian stance relate to a passionate style of life and thought (p. 17)?

1.8 Evaluate "inwardly" as the author suggests (p. 18). What characterizes your faith experience?

1.9 What two things can one do to renew spiritual passion (pp. 20–21)?

1.10 The author uses the strong words *passion* and *glow* to imply power. Write a challenge to yourself using these words.

2: Doing More and Enjoying It Less

2.1 Is the author's observation in the first paragraph (p. 22) true in your recent conversations?

2.2 Give two examples that support the author's descriptions of loss of passion due to the "joyless merry-go-round of activity" (pp. 25–26).

2.3 If you are in salaried Christian ministry or are an active layperson, how are you dealing with negative inner messages when you relax from church activities (p. 26)?

2.4 One cause for weariness is the Christian media glut (p. 27). Suggest several ways in which you purposely or unconsciously "close out" stimuli to prevent overload.

2.5 What two things may occur as a result of a relentless flow of information, religious stimulation and opportunity (p. 28)?

2.6   Write a statement relating to religious activities based on the following verses on Jesus lifestyle: Mark 1:12–20, 35, 45; 2:13, 15, 23; 3:7, 13, 19; 4:1, 10, 35; 5:21; 6:1, 30, 45–46; 7:24; 9:2; 13:3; 14:32.

2.7   Pose your own answers to the author's questions on page 31: Where does spiritual dullness come from? What are the consequences? What can we do about it? How might we avoid it?

2.8   The author mentions two types of fatigue (pp. 31–32). Which of these can you note in your life?

2.9   Read again the Scripture references in question 6 and comment on the level of Christ's passion (p. 32).

2.10   Imagine yourself "calm in spirit" (pp. 32–33). Describe your appearance in this image.

3: It's All Over!

3.1   Were you ever wise like the Boston runners (p. 34). Did you ever gather energy or passion ahead, parcel it out slowly, or renew it later on? Write about this time.

3.2   Read about Christ's followers in Mark 6:31–37 (pp. 34–35). What emotions do you think they were experiencing?

3.3   List the author's seven passion-threatening conditions (subheads, Chapters 3, 4, 5).

3.4   The author asks us how Elijah got "drained" on page 38. Make at least three observations about his condition from the Older Testament (pp. 38–41).

3.5   Add one of your "emotional and spiritual hangover" times to those of General William Booth and Howard Guinness (pp. 42–43). What did you do for renewal?

3.6   The author suggests scheduling a period before and after an intense assignment for renewal (p. 43). What plan might work for you?

4: Running on Empty

4.1   What is the difference between being "drained" and being "dried out" (pp. 45–46)?

4.2   Illustrate this difference from your personal experience.

4.3   Output without refueling seems to be foolish (pp. 46–48). Why do you think people are foolish in this way?

4.4   Read the accounts of David which are referred to on pages 48–49:
       a. His state before and during temptation (2 Samuel 11).
       b. Nathan's visit (2 Samuel 12:1–23).
       c. Psalms of remorse (Psalms 32, 38, 40, 51, 61, 63, 116).

4.5   If you have a hymnal, look through the contents

for selections that reflect an understanding of this dried-out condition. Make a list of some of the titles.

4.6   The author writes that more than two thousand persuasive messages are pressed at us each day (p. 51). Observe for one hour—either at your local mall or on television—for some attempts to distort the truth. Write your observations.

4.7   Read Genesis 13 and describe Lot's distorted views (pp. 53–54).

4.8   What are some of the "good experiences and opportunities" distorting you by oversensation (p. 54)?

4.9   What do you think the author means by an "independent base of judgment," and how can you use it (pp. 54–55)?

5: Further Threats to Spiritual Passion

5.1   Read about David's devastated condition (p. 58) in 2 Samuel 15:12–18; 16:13, 14.

5.2   What resulted after a devastating moment in your life? Were you stronger or depleted (p. 59)?

5.3   If the devastating condition depleted you, how might you have prevented such?

5.4   The author exposed his occasional disillusionment when his great dreams were deflated (pp. 60–61). Recall one of your disillusionments.

5.5   Fill in the blanks with your imagination, as the author suggested, and record your conclusion about Moses' state of passion in Exodus 2:11–15 and 4:18–31 (pp. 61–62).

5.6   The defeated condition is introduced in the Luke 22:54–61 account of Peter's failure (p. 63). What were his feelings?

5.7   If "passion does not dwell in the heart of the defeated" (p. 63), what *does* dwell in the defeated heart?

5.8   Identify a person in your life who may be your intimidator, a person who controls your mind or to whom you bow (p. 64).

5.9   In each of the following biblical accounts, comment on the state of intimidation:
a. Mark 14:50
b. Numbers 13:28–33
c. Isaiah 7:1–4; 8:5–13

5.10   Where are your "Harvard's" and "MIT's" (p. 65)? What must you tell yourself when a symbol of visible power intimidates you (p. 68)?

5.11   Consider Gilkey's monologues once more (pp. 66–68). What would you answer in defense of your position?

5.12   Review by listing the seven conditions that

threaten spiritual passion (pp. 37–68). Circle any that confront you now.

6: Those Who Bring Joy

6.1 The author described personal energy loss or gain due to interaction with people (pp. 69–70). Write briefly about a time when you *gained* energy in an interaction.

6.2 Now write briefly about a time when you *lost* energy in an interaction.

6.3 What are the five kinds of people that affect spiritual passion? (subheads, Chapters 6, 7).

6.4 Monitoring the process of working with people means what two tasks (p. 71)?

6.5 Examine the VRP's (pp. 71–74) in your life. Identify one or two and give some clues about their energizing role.

6.6 Who are the VIP's (pp. 74–76) who share your passion? What do you need to realize in order to minimize conflict?

6.7 Do you have, or could you nurture, a John Riland person (pp. 75–76) to whom you could be accountable? Discuss any reservations which you have.

6.8 Write out and memorize 2 Timothy 2:2. Now place a few possible names of VTP's (pp. 76–77) with the verse.

7: The Happy and the Hurting

7.1 Write a short paragraph of challenge to VNP's (pp. 78–82) inviting them to a new level as VTP's.

7.2 Do you agree that "no one can remain forever in the presence of Christ and be a VNP" (p. 79)? Comment.

7.3 The author says that "most of our heavy expenditures are for the very nice people" in church life (p. 80). Evaluate that statement on the basis of your expectations for how the church should spend its money.

7.4 If you concur with the author's social theory that people draw near to roles rather than to the person (p. 81), suggest some correctives in church teaching and behavior.

7.5 What language have you used to identify the very draining people (p. 82)?

7.6 Can you discern any traits or relational patterns that might identify you as a draining person to another Christian (p. 83)?

7.7 Read:
   a. 1 Corinthians 5 (the immoral church member).
   b. Philippians 4:2–7 (Euodias and Syntyche).
   c. Joshua 7:1–26 (Achan).
   d. Nehemiah 13 (critics, slow movers, men with hidden agendas).
   e. Judges 6 (Gideon).

228

7.8   What three important things must we understand about VDP's (p. 85)? Would you add to these or change any?

7.9   By making yourself continually available to the VNP's and the VDP's, are you teaching, feeding, and providing dependence, as the author suggests (pp. 86–87)?

7.10 Note the dilemma posed at the end of Chapter 7. Why is it a good idea to "think twice" before turning your back upon a VDP (pp. 87–88)?

8: Friendly Fire

8.1   Restate the author's main point in your words from the account of Vietnam (pp. 89–90) and the story of Samson (pp. 90–91).

8.2   What is necessary to maintain or renew our spiritual passion (p. 91)?

8.3   Identify the four spirits that destroy spiritual passion (subheads, pp. 93–100). Can you add others?

8.4   In 3 John 9, what choice did Diotrephes make in relation to other workers (p. 93)? What was the result?

8.5   Passion can subside because of a competitive spirit, according to the author (pp. 94–97). List two of his five illustrations from human experience, and add one of your own.

8.6   The author tells about his experience with some missionaries in another country to illustrate "energy nullified by a critical spirit" (pp. 98–99). Can you add another dimension to this case? Can you support or rationalize the missionaries' behavior with the use of Scripture?

8.7   Check some of your recent encounters with people. Write down any of your attempts to impress them (p. 99). Assess whether these attempts may indicate a pattern of yours.

8.8   How can you avoid the vain spirit (pp. 99–100)?

8.9   Locate some Scripture verses that support the author's statement that Spiritual passion cannot coexist with resentments (p. 102).

8.10   Meditate on the image of the dispirited soldier (p. 102). Do you see any likeness of yourself? Write a plan for dealing with the poisoned spirits you find within yourself.

9: He Knew I Couldn't Handle It!

9.1   The idea of original sin (p. 103) and its power in one's life is not popular. Write a brief argument, citing Scripture, to support the author's viewpoint that "weariness results from being constantly ambushed by that power."

9.2   The third origin of spiritual tiredness experienced by Bowen and Fénelon (pp. 103–104) is warfare in the inner world of a person. Describe an experience you may have had that seemed like struggle from within.

9.3   Give several examples of *acceptable* ambition in the majority of vocations or jobs; in contrast, give some examples of *unacceptable* ambition in the leadership in the church (p. 106).

9.4   Shine the light on your inner world (p. 107). If ambition is lurking there, how does it show itself?

9.5   Personal ambition and the spiritually passionate desire to advance the interest of Christ are closely paralleled, according to the author (p. 106). How might one discern the difference? Further, how might healing come to the weary ambitious (pp. 107–109)?

9.6   Ambition's twin sister, pride, was recognized as a problem by the Bible teacher (p. 109). How does the author suggest that we deal with pride and ambition (p. 111)?

10: It's What's Inside That Counts

10.1   Describe your observations about committed Christians who burn out (pp. 113–114). Why does the author propose that the wholesale fatigue among evangelicals may be a relatively new phenomenon?

10.2   What are some of the remedies many people prescribe for the epidemic described (p. 114)?

231

10.3   Why does a "wholesale exhaustion of the spirit" exist today (pp. 114–115)?

10.4   What insight does the author mention for discovering secrets to renew spiritual passion (p. 116)?

10.5   Before continuing any further, write some ideas you might propose for renewing spiritual passion.

11: Rack 'Em Up

11.1   Think of at least one biblical example of a dream developed and then dissipated (p. 119).

11.2   State the author's key word for renewal (p. 120). Would you substitute a word that has more meaning for you?

11.3   What are the three major themes in which the recollection process happens (p. 121)?

11.4   The author offers answers in response to questions about the recollection process (pp. 121–122). State the answers in your own words.

11.5   How does your answer to question 11.4 compare with your answer to question 10.5?

12: Safe Places

12.1   What was David looking for in a safe place (pp. 124–126)? Recall some green pastures, or safe places, that you have experienced.

12.2   Do your safe places resemble an Eden (p. 126)?
        Write an invitation to a weary pilgrim to come to
        your Eden, and describe the difference or sim-
        ilarity.

12.3   Briefly write about three Older Testament ac-
        counts of safe places (pp. 126–128).

12.4   Safe places in biblical history are:
        a. The Tabernacle (Exodus 26–30).
        b. The Temple (1 Kings 5:3–8:21; Hebrews
           9:1–10).
        c. The Temple in Jerusalem (Matthew 17:24–27;
           Mark 11:15–19).
        Read the accounts of these safe places and note if
        they describe places of protection, rest, or re-direc-
        tion.

12.5   Expand the author's creative listing of safe places.
        He moves from cathedrals, churches, and her-
        mitages (pp. 128–131) to momentary safe places
        (p. 132). Where are your safe places?

12.6   If you are drained and realize that you have no
        easily available safe place, how might you *create* an
        "instant" safe place (pp. 132–133)?

13: The Place of Secrets

13.1   What aspects of God's nature does David disclose
        in Psalm 63 (pp. 136–137)?

13.2   Describe times when you have felt need or stress to
        the degree which David expressed in Psalm 63.

13.3　In his sanctuary, David's fear was abated (p. 138). Describe what you think happens at such times.

13.4　Daniel 2:20–23 tells of Daniel's talk to God in his sanctuary (p. 138), and Acts 4:24–26 of Peter and John's talk to God in theirs (pp. 138–139). What relevance do their speeches have for us?

13.5　Memorize Jeremiah's words in Lamentations 3:23 (p. 139). Find the clue to a portion of David's secret.

13.6　Can you recall any "night room" helps (pp. 141–142) in your life?

13.7　What do wings (pp. 142–144) symbolize to you? What symbol of protection do you use?

13.8　Have you known a strong hand (pp. 145–147) in your life as described in Psalms 18:35; 63:8; 73:23? Write about your experience. If you have not experienced a strong hand, imagine yourself reaching out to grasp God's hand (p. 148).

13.9　Name your personal safe place at home and your personal safe place at work (p. 149). If you haven't established these safe places, institute them for trial this week.

13.10　What surroundings (colors, items, structures) are best for you in your safe places at home and at work (p. 151)? Why?

13.11   What could you add to your sanctuary to enhance the feeling of safety?

14: The Still Times

14.1   Restate the author's "only answer to an exhausted, passionless life" (p. 155) to make it more personal.

14.2   How would you advise men and women who believe that "personal worth is built upon what they do rather than what they are" (pp. 156–157)?

14.3   Does the author have sound basis for concluding that God brought each phase of His work to completion with a still time to study and evaluate? Write his point (pp. 158–159).

14.4   How does observance of Sabbath guard against workaholism (p. 162)? What have you learned about this in your experience?

14.5   Do you agree or disagree with the author's assertion that "it is virtually impossible for a person to become an obsessive hoarder of material things when the tithe is built in as a discipline" (p. 162)?

14.6   Interview a friend from another faith tradition about Sabbath observance (p. 162). Record your explanation of the *principle* of still time.

14.7   If there is a lesson in the entire household re-
        nouncing work on the Sabbath (pp. 163–164),
        how can this lesson be applied to your present
        church? Suggest a specific plan of action.

14.8   Name some instances of times when you sub-
        stituted amusement and leisure for genuine rest (p.
        165).

14.9   Noting Ruth Graham's example (p. 167), what can
        you do to "create the Sabbathing moment"?

14.10   Write a resolve for *your* life, for example: "Mark the
        map of your life with frequent safe places, and the
        calendar of your life with sabbaths or still times."

15: Special Friends

15.1   Give an example, from your own experience or
        from the media, of people who drain each other
        (pp. 168–169). Now, give an example of a group
        of special friends who support each other (p. 171).
        Make several observations about each group.

15.2   The author indicates that certain people are an
        indispensable part of the economy of spiritual pas-
        sion (pp. 171–175). Who are these people? Com-
        ment on the accuracy of the author's observation
        from your personal experience.

15.3   How do you feel about having a sponsor in your
        spiritual journey (pp. 175–176)?

15.4   Do you agree that Mordecai was Esther's sponsor (pp. 176–178)? If you agree, what was specifically accomplished by this relationship?

15.5   Identify a New Testament example of sponsorship (p. 179) and elaborate on the outcome.

15.6   Write the author's definition of affirmation (p. 180). Now choose a Christian whom you know you should affirm. Keeping the definition in mind, make a list of things you could do and words you could say that would express caring and affirmation to this Christian brother or sister.

15.7   Fill in this Special Friends Inventory:

a. Your sponsor(s) _____
b. Your affirmer(s) _____
c. Someone to whom you are sponsor _____
d. Someone whom you affirm _____

16: More Special Friends

16.1   "No one grows where truth is absent" is the author's premise for encouraging openness to rebuke and criticism (p. 186). How do you think *you* should respond to rebuke and criticism (p. 188)?

16.2   Isolate a time when you were rebuked. What resulted? Did your response fit the answer you gave to question 16.1?

16.3   List a few true friends who presently need your word of rebuke. Read Armstrong's rebuke of the author (p. 188) and Edwards' rebuke of Simeon (pp. 189–190), and then write a gentle approach you might use for at least one of your friends.

16.4   Some anecdotes (pp. 191–193) are given to illustrate the importance of intercession. Write a few sentences about the importance of intercession in your life. Who are your intercessors?

16.5   Draw out of the material on partners various qualities or actions characterizing a vitalizing partnership (Hudson and Maria Taylor, p. 195; Hoste and Smith, pp. 195–196; Paul and Barnabas, pp. 196–197; Hopkins and Roosevelt, pp. 197–198).

16.6   What personal application do you feel you should make regarding intercession or partnership?

16.7   Write your story of a tender person who helped make sense out of your life (pp. 198–200).

17: Renewing Your Spiritual Passion

17.1   Note the title of this chapter. The *ing* indicates action and process. On a scale of 1–10, where would you rate your present level of spiritual passion? Read the dynamite box story (p. 201) for help in determining your rating.

17.2   How does the author distinguish *weariness* from *stress* or *burnout* (p. 202)?

17.3   Write a hypothetical description of a tired and weary fellow Christian. Now prescribe a specific safe place, a specific means for still time, and a specific special friend category for that person (p. 203).

17.4   The author asks what the spiritually passionate life looks like (p. 205). Write a paragraph in answer to his question.

17.5   Read the account in 1 Chronicles 11 about David. What three truths found in this story help put the Christian life in perspective (subheads, pp. 207–211)?

17.6   Reflect and write several one-sentence thoughts on the wishes of God (pp. 207–209). "The wish of God is . . ." Include some of the author's most helpful statements.

17.7   What were the actions chosen by John the Baptist, Peter, Paul, Mary, and General Booth (pp. 210-211)? Now identify a choice facing you out of your safe-place and still-time awarenesses.

17.8   How does the author relate the normal life experience of the first man and woman to the model life of spiritual passion (p. 212)?

17.9   Describe the kind of passion we need today (p. 215). What changes will you effect in your own life to attain this passion?

Gordon MacDonald's best-loved works can now be found in **The Gordon MacDonald Bestseller Series**, each including a study guide for individual or group use. Look for the following other titles in the series:

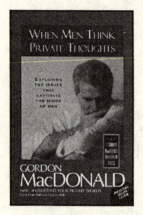

When Men Think Private Thoughts

MacDonald addresses the questions men often ask of themselves, exploring avenues that include sexuality and masculinity; intimacy, romance, and friendship; and achievement and definitions of success, revealing how each road intersects with a man's soul. Readers will be able to put aside the stereotypical definitions of maleness that plague men's private thoughts and will see instead a Christ-centered model. This book was designed for men, but will also help women better understand the men they love.

0-7852-7163-5 • Trade Paperback • $12.99 • 288 pages

The Life God Blesses

MacDonald asks readers if they are prepared for the storms of life, or if they are more concerned with outward appearances than with what lies beneath the surface in their soul. Skillfully, he leads readers through the steps necessary to develop a mature soul and to recognize and receive God's blessings.

0-7852-7160-0 • Trade Paperback • $12.99 • 276 pages

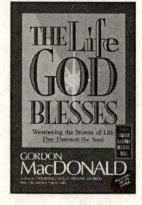

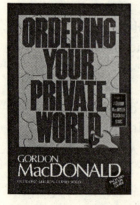

Ordering Your Private World

This bestseller has already helped over a million readers find a sense of being satisfied from the inside out. By working through five specific areas—motivation, use of time, wisdom and knowledge, spiritual strength, and restoration—MacDonald gives readers helpful advice for fighting the disorder within and experiencing personal growth and spiritual development.

0-7852-7161-9 • Trade Paperback • $12.99 • 228 pages